TWENTY-FIRST CENTURY
WARPLANES

THE WORLD'S MOST POTENT MILITARY AIRCRAFT

TWENTY-FIRST CENTURY
WARPLANES

THE WORLD'S MOST POTENT MILITARY AIRCRAFT

Steve Crawford

MBI Publishing Company

Library of Congress Cataloging-in-Publication Data Available.

ISBN 0-7603-1407-1

Printed in Hong Kong

Editorial and design
Brown Partworks Limited
8 Chapel Place
Rivington Street
London
EC2A 3DQ
UK

Editor: Laura Collins
Picture research: Andrew Webb
Design: Richard Berry
Production: Matt Weyland

CONTENTS

ARGENTINA 6

CHINA 7

EUROPEAN COLLABORATION . . 9

FRANCE 18

GREAT BRITAIN 24

ISRAEL 32

JAPAN 33

RUSSIA 34

SPAIN 48

SWEDEN 49

TAIWAN 52

UNITED STATES 53

INDEX 96

AT-63 PAMPA

The Pampa is a single-engine, high-wing advance pilot trainer. Nineteen aircraft were originally built during the 1980s by Fabrica Militar de Aviones, the Argentine military depot that was privatized by the American company Lockheed Martin in 1995. Today there are 16 Pampas in service with the Argentine Air Force, which are deployed as part of the Air Training Command (the Argentinian Air Force consists of eight air brigades). The Pampas serve with *Escuadron de Caza 1*, which operates from Mendoza and El Plumerillo air bases. With a fully upgraded cockpit and modern avionics suite, the new AT-63 under production in Argentina is setting a new standard for a low-cost basic training aircraft, one which can also be used as an advanced trainer and light attack aircraft. The Argentine Air Force has contracted to build 12 AT-63s. On 19 June 2001, Lockheed Martin presented this new aircraft during the Paris Air Show and is now offering it to customers worldwide. The new generation AT-63 maintains the ease of maintenance and airframe stability of the original version, produced in the late 1980s as the IA-63, while adding advanced upgrades and additional combat capabilities. The latest Pampa certainly ranks alongside the Hawk and Alpha as an effective trainer and light attack aircraft.

SPECIFICATIONS

Primary Role:	advanced trainer
Crew:	2
Contractor:	Lockheed Martin
Length:	10.9m (33.22ft)
Wingspan:	9.68m (31.75ft)
Height:	4.29m (14.1ft)
Maximum Take-off Weight:	3800kg (8377lb)
Powerplant:	1 x TFE-731-2C turbofan
Thrust:	1591kg (3500lb)
Maximum Speed:	750km/h (466mph)
Ceiling:	12,900m (42,323ft)
Range:	1500km (937 miles)
Armament:	1 x 30mm cannon pod
Systems:	1553B data bus, INS/GPS
Date Deployed:	2001

JH-7

This twin-engined, two-seat, swept-back, high-mounted wing supersonic fighter-bomber is designed to have the same role and configuration class as the Russian Sukhoi Su-24 Fencer. It has high mounted wings with compound sweepback and dog tooth leading edges; twin turbofans with lateral air intakes; all-swept tail surface, comprising large main fin, single small ventral fin and low set, all-moving tailplane; and a small overwing fence at approximately two-third span. Armament includes a twin-barrel 23mm gun in the nose, two stores pylons under each wing, plus a rail for close-range air-to-air missile (AAMs) at each wingtip. Typical underwing load for maritime attack includes two C-801 sea-skimming anti-ship missiles (ASMs) and two drop tanks. Though the JH-7 has provided the Chinese Navy with improved attack capabilities, the WS9 turbofan does not have enough thrust to equal foreign aircraft in the same weight class in terms of payload delivery. The Chinese plan is to use Russian-made engines and advanced composite materials to improve the aircraft and equip it with terrain-tracking radar and electronic countermeasures equipment. This improved JH-7A will have more reliable AL-31F engines and a radar with a detection range of 100km (62 miles) and the ability to simultaneously track 14 targets and attack 4 to 6.

SPECIFICATIONS

Primary Role:	*fighter-bomber*
Crew:	*2*
Contractor:	*Xian Aircraft Industry Company*
Length:	*21m (68.89ft)*
Wingspan:	*12.80m (42ft)*
Height:	*6.22m (20.4ft)*
Maximum Take-off Weight:	*27,415kg (60,439lb)*
Powerplant:	*2 x Xian WS9 turbofans*
Thrust:	*9325kg (20,515lb) each*
Maximum Speed:	*1808km/h (1122mph)*
Ceiling:	*15,500m (50,850ft)*
Range:	*900km (560 miles)*
Armament:	*2 x 23mm cannon, wingtip rails for PL-5 AAMs, 2 x C-801 or C-802 (YJ-1) ASMs*
Systems:	*unknown*
Date Deployed:	*1993*

J-8IIM FINBACK

The J-8 was the first Chinese Air Force jet fighter of domestic design. The overall configuration is a rather straightforward enlargement of the MiG-21/J-7 layout to accommodate two engines. Although it resembled Mikoyan's experimental Ye-152A, contrary to some early reports it was not based on that aircraft. Production began in December 1979, with about 100–150 units of the first configuration entering service. Design work on the improved J-8-2 began in 1980, with production beginning in late 1980. The Jian-8IIM upgrader, co-developed by China and Russia, is the result of a thorough modernization of the F-8M fighter ("M" standing for export-only weaponry in China's weapon designation system). The first flight of this version was conducted on 31 March 1996. It features upgraded electronics systems, the lack of which has disadvantaged China's fighter planes for a long time. The J-8IIM fighter will probably be equipped with Russia's or China's helmet sight and advanced PL-9 and P-73 missiles. Phazotron, a Russian firm, has agreed to provide 150–200 improved Zhuk radars mainly in support of China's new F-8II fighter. These radars can track while scanning on 24 targets, display up to 8 of them, and simultaneously provide fire-control solutions for 2–4 of them.

SPECIFICATIONS

Primary Role:	*interceptor*
Crew:	*1*
Contractor:	*Shenyang Aircraft Company*
Length:	*21.6m (70.9ft)*
Wingspan:	*9.3m (30ft)*
Height:	*5.4m (17.75ft)*
Maximum Take-off Weight:	*17,800kg (39,200lb)*
Powerplant:	*2 x Wopen 13A-II turbojets*
Thrust:	*6734kg (14,815lb) each*
Maximum Speed:	*2340km/h (1450mph)*
Ceiling:	*20,000m (65,616ft)*
Range:	*1300km (813 miles)*
Armament:	*2 x 23mm cannon, 4 x PL-2 or PL-7*
Systems:	*Izmurd ranging radar*
Date Deployed:	*1979*

ALPHA JET

The Dassault-Breguet-Dornier Alpha Jet is a twin-seat subsonic fighter-bomber that due to its conception and versatile characteristics is particularly suitable for supporting air offensive operations, ground operations, as well as for advanced training on bombers, fighters and operational conversion training, with the capability of using different weapon configurations. Its equipment allows it to obtain great efficiency when planning and executing missions. The Head-Up Display (HUD) saves the pilot from looking down into the cockpit to read the instruments, by superimposing data on a clear plate mounted at eye level. The navigation and fire-control computers are precise and permit great flexibility on attack missions. The use of the "AFA" computer makes the planning of a mission simpler, quicker and more efficient. The Alpha Jet 2 is a development of the training aircraft and is optimized for ground attack. It has an integrated weapon system – laser range finder, inertial navigation unit, HUD – allowing it to fulfil either weapon system training missions or ground-attack missions with a great accuracy. The Alpha Jet ATS (Advanced Training System) allows pilots to familiarize themselves with the navigation and attack systems of the latest and future European fighter aircraft.

SPECIFICATIONS

Primary Role:	light attack, advanced trainer
Crew:	2
Contractor:	Dassault-Breguet-Dornier
Length:	12.3m (40.25ft)
Wingspan:	9.14m (30ft)
Height:	4.19m (13ft)
Maximum Take-off Weight:	8000kg (17,637lb)
Powerplant:	2 x SNECMA 04-C6 turbofans
Thrust:	2705kg (5952lb) each
Maximum Speed:	1160km/h (725mph)
Ceiling:	15,240m (50,000ft)
Range:	2600km (1625 miles)
Armament:	mixture of Bl755, Matra F1 gun pod, Belouga, AGM-65 maverick, AIM-9L
Systems:	Radar Warning Receiver (RWR)
Date Deployed:	1977

AMX

The AMX, a joint programme undertaken by Alenia, Aermacchi and Embraer, is an attack aircraft for battlefield interdiction, close air support and reconnaissance. The wings are mounted high, swept back and tapered with square tips. AAMs are usually mounted on the wings. There are two air intakes forward of the wing roots; there is a single exhaust. The fuselage has a pointed nose and bubble canopy. The body widens at the air intakes and tapers to the rear. The tail flats are mid-mounted on the fuselage, swept back and tapered. It is capable of operating at high subsonic speed and low altitude, by day or night, and if necessary from bases with poorly equipped or damaged runways. Its low infrared signature, reduced radar equivalent cross-section and low vulnerability of structure and systems guarantee a high probability of mission success. The integrated ECM, air-to-air missiles and nose-mounted guns provide self-defence capabilities. The AMX-T is a twin-seater, high performance transonic turbofan jet, specifically developed for advanced and fighter lead-in training. It maintains the operational characteristics of the AMX, which is already in operation with the Brazilian and Italian air forces. The AMX-T was selected by the Venezuelan Air Force to replace the old T-2A Buckeyes in the advanced training role.

SPECIFICATIONS

Primary Role:	*light bomber/fighter*
Crew:	*1*
Contractor:	*Alenia, Aermacchi, Embraer*
Length:	*13.58m (44.5ft)*
Wingspan:	*8.84m (29ft)*
Height:	*4.54m (14.92ft)*
Maximum Take-off Weight:	*13,027kg (28,660lb)*
Powerplant:	*1 x Rolls-Royce Spey MK 807*
Thrust:	*5010kg (11,023lb)*
Maximum Speed:	*1053km/h (658mph)*
Ceiling:	*13,000m (42650ft)*
Range:	*1840km (1150 miles)*
Armament:	*1 x 20mm cannon, AIM-9L Sidewinder, ELT-555 jamming pod, Belouga, Kormoran*
Systems:	*FIAR Pointer range-only radar, RWR, ballistic bombsight*
Date Deployed:	*1989*

C-160 TRANSALL

The Transall C-160 first flew in 1963. Production was completed in 1972, but in 1977 the programme was reinstated to produce a "new generation" C-160 for France. The last of these new generation aircraft entered service in 1987. Two turboprop engines are mounted under and extend beyond the wings' leading edges. The fuselage is long, thick and tapered to the rear with a round, solid nose, stepped cockpit and upswept tail section. The tail flats are mid-mounted on a thinned body, equally tapered with blunt tips. The fin is tall and tapered with a blunt tip and a fairing in the leading edge. A variant is the C-160 Gabriel, which features an ELINT subsystem provided by Thomson-CSF Radars & Contre-Mesures for detection, analysis and location of radar sources with a subsystem for detection, interception, classification, listening-in, analysis and location of radio transmitters. Four communications relay aircraft, designation C-160H Astarte, have been delivered to the French Air Force since 1987. The aircrafts' main mission is communications with the submerged nuclear ballistic missile submarines of the French fleet. The aircraft are equipped with unjammable VLF communications including a Rockwell VLF transmitter and a Thales communications centre. The VLF system includes dual trailing wire antennae.

SPECIFICATIONS

Primary Role:	transport, EW, surveillance
Crew:	5
Contractor:	Aerospatiale
Length:	32.4m (106.25ft)
Wingspan:	40m (131.25ft)
Height:	11.67m (38.28ft)
Maximum Take-off Weight:	51,000kg (112,200lb)
Powerplant:	2 x Rolls-Royce Tyne 22
Thrust:	4549kg (10,007lb) each
Maximum Speed:	515km/h (322mph)
Ceiling:	7925m (26,000ft)
Range:	5095km (3184 miles)
Armament:	usually none
Systems:	inertial navigation system, GPS, ELINT, VLF
Date Deployed:	1963

CN-235

The CN-235 is a high-wing, pressurized, twin turbo-prop aircraft with short take-off and landing (STOL) performance that can carry a maximum payload of 6000kg (13,200lb). The CN-235 has been conceived for tactical military transport and is capable of operating from unpaved runways and has excellent low-level flying characteristics for tactical penetration. It can be used to transport up to 48 paratroopers who can exit via either of the two side doors or the rear ramp. The CN-235 is able to carry out high- and low-altitude in-flight drops to forward troops. On medical evacuation missions, the aircraft can transport up to 21 stretchers, plus four medics. Although the CN-235 was initially the result of cooperation between CASA and ITPN of Indonesia, CASA has developed its own series and versions, with increases in weights and performance. CASA's aircraft is thus the product of continuous development, not just in the military sphere, but also in civil areas. The CN-235 is the ideal platform for the development and integration of a wide variety of versions, such as the Maritime Patrol Version (Persuader), electronic warfare, early warning and photo reconnaissance. The CN-235 is undoubtedly a leader in its class, with more than 220 aircraft sold to 29 operators and 500,000 flight hours to date.

SPECIFICATIONS

Primary Role:	light transport
Crew:	3
Contractor:	CASA and ITPN
Length:	21.40m (70.1ft)
Wingspan:	25.81m (84.66ft)
Height:	8.2m (26.9ft)
Maximum Take-off Weight:	16,500kg (36,376lb)
Powerplant:	2 x General Electric CT7-9C turboprops
Thrust:	2610kg (5742lb) each
Maximum Speed:	445km/h (276mph)
Ceiling:	9900m (32,480ft)
Range:	5000km (3125 miles)
Armament:	none
Systems:	ESM/ECM and ELINT/COMINT
Date Deployed:	1986

EUROFIGHTER TYPHOON

Eurofighter is a single-seat, twin-engine combat aircraft which will be used in the air-to-air, air-to-ground and tactical reconnaissance roles. Its design is optimized for air dominance performance with high instantaneous and sustained turn rates, and specific excess power. Special emphasis has been placed on low wing loading, high thrust-to-weight ratio, excellent all-round vision and carefree handling. Eurofighter's high performance is matched by excellent all-round vision and by sophisticated attack, identification and defence systems which include the ECR 90 long-range radar and Infrared Search and Track (IRST) system, advanced medium- and short-range air-to-air missiles and a comprehensive electronic warfare suite. The aircraft is intentionally aerodynamically unstable to provide extremely high levels of agility, reduced drag and enhanced lift. The unstable design cannot be flown by conventional means and the pilot controls the aircraft via a computerised "fly-by-wire" system. The Eurojet EJ200 turbofan engine combines high thrust with low fuel consumption. To reduce ownership costs over Eurofighter Typhoon's in-service life of 25 years or 6000 flying hours, and to ensure maximum availability, the areas of reliability, maintainability and testability have been given equal priority to performance and flight safety.

SPECIFICATIONS

Primary Role:	*multirole fighter*
Crew:	*1*
Contractor:	*BAe, DASA, Alenia, CASA*
Length:	*14.96m (49ft)*
Wingspan:	*10.95m (35.9ft)*
Height:	*5.28m (17.32ft)*
Maximum Take-off Weight:	*21,000kg (46,200lb)*
Powerplant:	*2 x EJ200 turbofans*
Thrust:	*9091kg (20,000lb) each*
Maximum Speed:	*2125km/hr (1328mph)*
Ceiling:	*classified*
Range:	*1389km (868 miles)*
Armament:	*1 x 27mm gun, mix of BVRAAM, SRAAM ,laser-guided bombs, anti-armour weapons*
Systems:	*ECR 90 radar, IRST*
Date Deployed:	*2002*

JAGUAR

The Jaguar has a long sleek fuselage with a large swept tail fin and rudder. The fuselage features a long, pointed, chiselled nose, and the relatively short-span swept wings are shoulder-mounted on the fuselage. The internal jet engines, mounted to the rear of the cockpit, have rectangular air intakes either side of the fuselage behind the cockpit, with their top surfaces forming an extension of the wing. The engine exhausts show prominently under the forward portion of the tail. The rear jetpipes are located forward and below the tailplane which has marked anhedral; the raised bubble canopy is set above the sharply pointed nose. The twin mainwheels of the undercarriage retract into the fuselage. A variety of weapons, including cluster, freefall, retard and laser-guided bombs, as well as rockets, can be carried. Two 30mm cannon are mounted internally. To mark targets for laser-guided weapons, the aircraft carries the thermal imaging and laser designation (TIALD) pod. For self-defence, Sidewinder infrared missiles are carried and the aircraft is fitted with comprehensive electronic countermeasures. With mission data fed into the computer, all the information for a pinpoint attack is relayed to the HUD. From the display, the pilot knows exactly where the target is located and when to release his weapons for maximum effect.

SPECIFICATIONS

Primary Role:	*close air support*
Crew:	*1*
Contractor:	*Dassault, BAe*
Length:	*16.83m (55.25ft)*
Wingspan:	*8.69m (28.5ft)*
Height:	*4.80m (15.74ft)*
Maximum Take-off Weight:	*15,000kg (33,000lb)*
Powerplant:	*2 x Adour 104 turbofans*
Thrust:	*3320kg (7305lb) each*
Maximum Speed:	*1593km/h (996mph)*
Ceiling:	*12,192m (40,000ft)*
Range:	*3524km (2202 miles)*
Armament:	*2 x 30mm guns, mix of Matra Magic R550 AAMs, AS 30 ASMs, rockets, bombs*
Systems:	*ECM, gyroscopic guidance*
Date Deployed:	*1972*

TORNADO F3

The Tornado is a twin-seat, twin-engined, variable geometry aircraft that is supersonic at all altitudes. The wings of the aircraft are high-mounted, variable, swept-back and tapered with angular, blunt tips. There are two turbofan engines inside the body. The air intakes are diagonal and box-like alongside the fuselage forward of the wing roots. There are twin exhausts. The fuselage is solid and has a needle nose. The body thickens midsection and tapers to the tail section. The tail is tall, swept-back and has a tapered fin with a curved tip and a step in the leading edge. The flats are large, mid-mounted on the body, swept-back and tapered with blunt tips. The Tornado F3 air defence fighter has an 80 percent commonality with the Tornado GR1 strike/attack aircraft. The Tornado F3 is optimized for long-range interception, for which it carries four Skyflash radar-guided missiles and four AIM 9 Sidewinder infrared AAMs, plus internally mounted 27mm Mauser cannons. Tornado F3s are being equipped with the new Joint Tactical Information Distribution System. Operating in conjunction with E-3D Sentry airborne early warning aircraft and other allied fighters, the crew can thus select its own target and move to within "kill" distance without using the fighter's own search radar until the very last moment.

SPECIFICATIONS

Primary Role:	*air defence fighter*
Crew:	*2*
Contractor:	*Panavia Aircraft GmbH*
Length:	*16.72m (54.85ft)*
Wingspan:	*13.91m (45.63ft) fully forward*
Height:	*5.95m (19.52ft)*
Maximum Take-off Weight:	*28,000kg (61,600lb)*
Powerplant:	*2 x RB199-34R turbofans*
Thrust:	*6582kg (14,480lb) each*
Maximum Speed:	*2336km/h (1452mph)*
Ceiling:	*15,240m (50,000ft)*
Range:	*3900km (2437 miles)*
Armament:	*2 x 27mm cannon, Sidewinder, HARM, AGM-65, ALARM, Paveway, Apache,*
Systems:	*Joint Tactical Information Distribution System*
Date Deployed:	*1984*

TORNADO GR1

The GR1 originated from a UK Staff Requirement in 1969 which called for a medium-range, low-level, counter-air strike aircraft, with the further capabilities of interdiction and reconnaissance. The Tornado first saw action during the Gulf War of 1991, when several were lost as a result of daring ultra-low-level missions to close Iraqi airfields. The proliferation of anti-aircraft defences in Iraq, Bosnia and elsewhere that the UK might be called on to operate in has meant that the standard GR1 is in danger of not being able to fulfil the covert deep-penetration operations that it was designed for. Furthermore, the advance of air-delivered weapons has meant that strike aircraft need to become ever more sophisticated, especially given the fears of "collateral damage" or accidentally hitting civilian targets. The Tornado GR1 strike/attack aircraft is capable of carrying a wide range of conventional stores, including the JP233 anti-airfield weapon, the ALARM anti-radar missile and laser-guided bombs. The reconnaissance version, designated the GR1A, retains the full operational capability of the GR1. The GR1B, equipped with Sea Eagle air-to-surface missiles, undertakes the anti-surface shipping role. For self-defence, the Tornado carries Sidewinder air-to-air missiles and is fitted with twin internal 27mm cannons.

SPECIFICATIONS

Primary Role:	strike/attack aircraft
Crew:	2
Contractor:	Panavia Aircraft GmbH
Length:	16.72m (54.85ft)
Wingspan:	13.91m (45.63ft) fully forward
Height:	5.95m (19.52ft)
Maximum Take-off Weight:	28,000kg (61,600lb)
Powerplant:	2 x RB199-34R turbofans
Thrust:	6582kg (14,480lb) each
Maximum Speed:	2336km/h (1452mph)
Ceiling:	15,240m (50,000ft)
Range:	3900km (2418 miles)
Armament:	2 x 27mm cannon, Sidewinder, HARM, AGM-65, ALARM, Sea Eagle, Paveway, Apache, JP233
Systems:	Sideways Looking Infrared, Linescan surveillance system
Date Deployed:	1980

TORNADO GR4

A mid-life update (MLU) programme was completed by the end of 1998 which gave the aircraft the capability to carry advanced weapons such as the anti-armour weapon "Brimstone" and the stand-off attack missile "Storm Shadow". The updated aircraft is designated Tornado GR4. The last of the updates is scheduled for early 2003. The MLU will allow the RAF's Tornados to serve well into the twenty-first century. The airframe's life is to be extended as a result of more advanced technology and this will avoid the necessity of expensive refits or the acquisition of new aircraft. In addition to the existing range of weaponry, such as laser-guided bombs and anti-radar missiles, the GR4 will be able to operate new equipment and will also be capable of using the Sea Eagle anti-shipping missile; whereas only the relatively small number of Tornado GR1Bs are currently fitted for maritime strike. The actual payload, speed, altitude and other performance characteristics of the GR4 will remain much the same as for the GR1. What will change is the overall capability of the aircraft. The ability to see in the dark when using FLIR and NVGs will permit GR4s to fly at terrain-following height without navigation lights or radar emissions. This makes the GR4 more stealthy, enhancing its chances of covert deep penetration and mission survival.

SPECIFICATIONS

Primary Role:	*all-weather strike aircraft*
Crew:	*2*
Contractor:	*Panavia Aircraft GmbH*
Length:	*16.72m (54.85ft)*
Wingspan:	*13.91m (45.63ft) fully forward*
Height:	*5.95m (19.52ft)*
Maximum Take-off Weight:	*28,000kg (61,600lb)*
Powerplant:	*2 x RB199-34R turbofans*
Thrust:	*6582kg (14,480lb) each*
Maximum Speed:	*2336km/h (1452mph)*
Ceiling:	*15,240m (50,000ft)*
Range:	*3900km (2418 miles)*
Armament:	*2 x 27mm cannon, Sidewinder, HARM, AGM-65, ALARM, Sea Eagle, Paveway, Apache, JP233*
Systems:	*Forward-Looking Infrared (FLIR), Defensive Aids*
Date Deployed:	*1998*

MIRAGE IV

In the mid-1950s, the French decided to develop their own nuclear deterrent force. As with other nuclear powers, France would eventually develop land-based and submarine-based missiles, and a strategic bomber, the Mirage IV. Work that would lead to the Mirage IV began in 1957. Dassault met the French government requirement for a strategic bomber by scaling up the Mirage III 50 percent in linear dimensions, doubling weight and wing area. The prototype Mirage IV first flew in June 1959, and had Atar 09C engines and a taller fin than later production aircraft. The second prototype flew in October 1961. The weapon for which the Mirage IV was designed, the 60-kiloton AN-22 nuclear weapon, fits into a recess in the fuselage. This weapon was modified after late 1967 to be parachute-retarded, when it was realized that the Mirage IV would not be able to penetrate Soviet airspace at high altitude. The Mirage IV obtained a new lease on life in the bomber role when 18 were rebuilt as Mirage IVPs ("P" for "Penetration") to carry the ASMP stand-off missile instead of the AN-22. This meant a considerable upgrade of the aircraft's avionics and the addition of a centre pylon to handle the ASMP. By 2000, all Mirage IV bombers had been retired, but five Mirage IVR variants remained in service.

SPECIFICATIONS

Primary Role:	*bomber/reconnaissance aircraft*
Crew:	*2*
Contractor:	*Dassault*
Length:	*23.50m (77.1ft)*
Wingspan:	*11.85m (38.9ft)*
Height:	*5.65m (18.5ft)*
Maximum Take-off Weight:	*31,600kg (70,000lb)*
Powerplant:	*2 x Atar 9K-50 turbojets*
Thrust:	*14,430kg (31,746lb) each*
Maximum Speed:	*2335km/h (1451mph)*
Ceiling:	*20,000m (65,600ft)*
Range:	*3200km (2000 miles)*
Armament:	*60kt nuclear bomb, ASMP nuclear weapon, Martel ASMs, bombs, rockets*
Systems:	*Cytano II radar, RWR, Agave radar*
Date Deployed:	*1962*

MIRAGE 2000B & C

The wings of the Mirage 2000 are low-mounted, delta shaped with clipped tips. There is one turbofan engine mounted in the fuselage, semicircular air intakes alongside the fuselage forward of the wings, a large, single exhaust which protrudes past the tail, and the fuselage is tube-shaped with a pointed nose and bubble canopy. The fin is swept-back and tapered with a clipped tip. The aircraft are fitted with the RDI pulse doppler radar and Super 530D semi-active AAMs with look-down and shoot-down capability. They also feature Magic 2 heat-seeking air-to-air combat missiles and an integrated electronic warfare suite. They are multirole and can also carry out air-to-ground missions with conventional bombs and rockets, although this is only a secondary assignment for them under the current French Air Force structure. Mirage 2000C/Bs can be refuelled in flight and were deployed with coalition forces in the Gulf War, and in the Bosnia and Kosovo conflicts in the 1990s. The Mirage 2000-5F version is a Mirage 2000C upgraded to Mirage 2000-5 standard with the RDY multitarget/multishoot capability, active seeker Mica missiles, and new cockpit displays and processors. At the beginning of 2000, the last of 37 Mirage 2000-5Fs ordered on the current upgrade contract were delivered.

SPECIFICATIONS

Primary Role:	*multirole fighter*
Crew:	*1*
Contractor:	*Dassault*
Length:	*14.36m (47.1ft)*
Wingspan:	*9.13m (29.9ft)*
Height:	*5.2m (17ft)*
Maximum Take-off Weight:	*17,000kg (37,400lb)*
Powerplant:	*1 x SNECMA M53-P2 turbofan*
Thrust:	*9720kg (21,385lb)*
Maximum Speed:	*1220km/h (762mph)*
Ceiling:	*16,500m (54,133ft)*
Range:	*3704km (2315 miles)*
Armament:	*2 x 30mm cannon, Super 530D, Magic 2 AAMs*
Systems:	*RDI pulse doppler radar, RDY multitarget/multishoot capability*
Date Deployed:	*1984*

MIRAGE 2000N

The Mirage 2000 strike aircraft is very similar to the Mirage III/5 and 50 variants, though it is not a variant of these aircraft but an entirely new model with advanced interceptor controls. In its secondary ground-attack role, the Mirage 2000 carries laser-guided missiles, rockets and bombs. The prime assignment of the two-seat Mirage 2000N is the nuclear strike mission, and as such has a dedicated WSO (weapon system operator) rear crew station to allow it to fulfil its strategic role. It features a special redundant navigation system with the Antilope terrain-following radar, allowing it to fly "blind" as low as 61m (200ft) above ground level under fully automatic guidance from the system. The cockpit is compatible with night vision goggles. The Mirage 2000N can be refuelled in flight and can also deliver unguided bombs and rockets as a secondary mission (the Mirage 2000D is a conventional strike derivative of the Mirage 2000N). Due to its strategic capabilities, the Mirage 2000N is not licensed for export. Laser-guided weapons can be delivered with the PDL-CT laser designator pod, which is fitted with an infrared camera. The Mirage 2000D is also able to carry out all-weather blind attacks on coordinates. Some 86 Mirage 2000Ds have been ordered by the French Air Force.

SPECIFICATIONS

Primary Role:	*nuclear strike aircraft*
Crew:	*2*
Contractor:	*Dassault*
Length:	*14.36m (47.11ft)*
Wingspan:	*9.13m (29.94ft)*
Height:	*5.30m (17.38ft)*
Maximum Take-off Weight:	*16,500kg (36,300lb)*
Powerplant:	*1 x SNECMA M 53 P2 turbofan*
Thrust:	*9700kg (21,340lb)*
Maximum Speed:	*2236km/h (1397mph)*
Ceiling:	*16,500m (54,133ft)*
Range:	*3335km (2084 miles)*
Armament:	*ASMP nuclear weapon*
Systems:	*fly-by-wire, inertial navigation systems, Antilope radar, GPS, integrated countermeasures, laser designator*
Date Deployed:	*1982*

MIRAGE F-1

ollowing on the Mirage F-2, which was a revival of the classic arrow-wing design with stabilizers, the Mirage F-1 is a defence and air superiority single-seater aircraft. This revival was made possible by technological advances which permit manufacture of ultra-thin but robust wings, enabling flight performance at supersonic speeds equivalent to that of delta wings (the wings are high-mounted, swept-back and tapered). The integrity of the fuselage structure allows the aircraft to carry a maximum amount of fuel. The Mirage F-1 prototype made its maiden flight on 23 December 1966, at Melun-Villaroche (the Seine-et-Marne region of France). Commissioned by the French Air Force in 1973, more than 700 Mirage F-1s have been sold to 11 countries. The Dassault Mirage F-1C was the standard French fighter before the Mirage 2000 entered service in the air force in 1984. Missiles are usually mounted at the wing tips. There is one turbojet engine in the body, semicircular air intakes alongside the body forward of the wing roots, and there is a single exhaust. The fuselage is long, slender, pointed nose with a blunt tail. There are two small belly fins under the tail section and a bubble canopy. The flats are mid-mounted on the fuselage, swept-back, and tapered with blunt tips. There is also a reconnaissance version, the F-1CR.

SPECIFICATIONS

Primary Role:	close air support/attack
Crew:	1
Contractor:	Dassault
Length:	14.94m (49ft)
Wingspan:	8.4m (27.6ft)
Height:	4.50m (14.76ft)
Maximum Take-off Weight:	16,200kg (35,640lb)
Powerplant:	1 x SNECMA Atar 9K50
Thrust:	6800kg (14,960kg)
Maximum Speed:	2238km/h (1390mph)
Ceiling:	15,850m (52,000ft)
Range:	1400km (875 miles)
Armament:	2 x 30mm cannon, Super 530, Magic 550, Sidewinder AAMs, AM 39 Exocet, AS.30L ASMs
Systems:	Cyrano IVM radar, RWR, Desire digital video recce pod, ECM
Date Deployed:	1973

RAFALE

The Rafale programme is composed of three versions of this multi-purpose aircraft: the single-seater (Rafale C), two-seater (Rafale B) and single-seater navy version (Rafale M). These three versions are fitted with the same engines, navigation and attack system, aircraft management system and flight control system. They are all able to perform all types of missions from ground-attack to air superiority. The first production aircraft flew for the first time on 4 December 1998, and total orders stand at 294 aircraft. Its excellent flying characteristics stem from the "delta-canard" aerodynamic concept combining a delta wing and an active foreplane judiciously located in relation to the wing so as to optimize aerodynamic efficiency and stability control without impeding the pilot's visibility. The Rafale C is a multirole fighter with a fully integrated weapons and navigation systems, making use of the latest technology and is capable of outstanding performance on multiple target air-to-air missions and air-to-surface missions deep behind enemy lines. The Rafale B retains most of the elements of the single-seater version, and its weapon and navigation system is exactly the same. The Rafale M also carries the same weapons. Designed for aircraft carriers, it retains most of the flying qualities of the other versions.

SPECIFICATIONS

Primary Role:	*multirole fighter*
Crew:	*1*
Contractor:	*Dassault*
Length:	*15.30m (50.2ft)*
Wingspan:	*10.9m (35.75ft)*
Height:	*5.34m (17.5ft)*
Maximum Take-off Weight:	*21,500kg (47,399lb)*
Powerplant:	*2 x SNECMA M88-2 turbofans*
Thrust:	*9954kg (21,900lb) each*
Maximum Speed:	*classified*
Ceiling:	*classified*
Range:	*3706km (2316 miles)*
Armament:	*1 X 30mm cannon, ASMP nuclear weapon, Mica AAMs, Exocet ASMs*
Systems:	*SPECTRA defensive system, RBE2 electronic scanning radar*
Date Deployed:	*2001*

SUPER ETENDARD

The Super Etendard is a carrier-based single-seat strike fighter first introduced into service in 1978. It is an updated version of the Etendard IVM. Based on experience gained during the Korean war (1950–53), the French authorities drew up specifications for a light interceptor aircraft. This definition was rapidly assimilated into a programme for a light tactical bomber that could also fulfil an air superiority mission. The naval single-seater combat aircraft, Dassault Super Etendard, is different to the Etendard IVM. Main modifications include updating of the weapons system through the installation (a first for a French production aircraft) of a modern navigation and combat management system. The aircraft prototype made its maiden flight on 28 October 1974 at Istres (the Bouches-du-Rhône region of France). The French Navy commissioned the plane for the first time in 1977, and 71 aircraft are now in service on the aircraft carriers *Foch* and *Clemenceau*. It was the Super Etendard, armed with Exocet anti-ship missiles and flown by Argentinian pilots (14 aircraft in all), that proved its combat effectiveness during the Falklands War with Britain in 1982. The Super Etendard will be replaced by the naval version of the Rafale multirole combat aircraft during the early years of the twenty-first century.

SPECIFICATIONS

Primary Role:	carrier-borne strike fighter
Crew:	1
Contractor:	Dassault
Length:	14.31m (46.9ft)
Wingspan:	9.6m (31.5ft)
Height:	3.86m (12.75ft)
Maximum Take-off Weight:	12,000kg (26,455lb)
Powerplant:	1 x SNECMA Atar turbojet
Thrust:	5011kg (11,025lb)
Maximum Speed:	1173km/h (733mph)
Ceiling:	13,700M (45,000ft)
Range:	1700km (1062 miles)
Armament:	2 x 30mm cannon, Magic 550 AAM, Exocet ASM
Systems:	Barracuda and Phimat jamming pods, Anémone radar. Drax radar detector
Date Deployed:	1978

CANBERRA PR9

The first jet bomber to serve with the Royal Air Force (RAF), the English Electric Canberra was designed with no defensive armament, relying instead on high speed, an operational ceiling of 14,630m (48,000ft) and great manoeuvrability to avoid opposing fighter aircraft. The fact that the Canberra is still in service today is testimony to the quality of the original design. Currently the RAF operates two versions of the aircraft, the T4 is a dual control trainer, and dedicated reconnaissance missions are undertaken by the venerable Canberra PR9, specialist aircraft that contribute significantly to meeting the RAF's reconnaissance task through the use of a wide range of onboard vertical and oblique cameras. The first RAF reconnaissance version, the PR3, first flew on 19 March 1950. The main difference between it and other Canberra versions was a 356mm (14in) extension to the forward fuselage to accommodate an additional fuel tank, a camera bay and a flare bay. Deliveries to the first squadron, No 540 at RAF Benson, began in December 1952. The PR7 was an improved version of the aircraft, but the definitive version was the PR9, which became operational with the RAF's No 58 Squadron. In 1962, PR9s were used to photograph Soviet shipping movements during the Cuban missile crisis.

SPECIFICATIONS

Primary Role:	*reconnaissance*
Crew:	*2*
Contractor:	*BAe*
Length:	*20.32m (66.6ft)*
Wingspan:	*20.67m (67.8ft)*
Height:	*4.77m (15.6ft)*
Maximum Take-off Weight:	*24,977kg (54,950lb)*
Powerplant:	*2 x Avon 109 turbojets*
Thrust:	*6741kg (14,800lb) each*
Maximum Speed:	*827km/h (517mph)*
Ceiling:	*14,630m (48,000ft)*
Range:	*5840km (3650 miles)*
Armament:	*none*
Systems:	*F49/F96 Mk4 Survey camera, LORAN air direction finder, ALQ-167 jamming suite, AIRPASS III Blue Parrot radar*
Date Deployed:	*1960*

HARRIER GR7

This is the latest in the long line of Harrier "Jump Jets" originating from the 1960s. The second-generation GR5 and GR7 versions replaced the original Harrier GR3s in the late 1980s and early 1990s. The GR7 is essentially a licence-built, American-designed AV-8B Harrier II fitted with RAF-specific systems as well as other changes, including additional underwing pylons for Sidewinder missiles. The improved design of the GR7 allows the aircraft to carry twice the load of a GR3 over the same distance or the same load twice the distance. The first flight of the Harrier GR7 was in 1989, and deliveries to RAF squadrons began in 1990. A total of 96 aircraft were ordered. Fully operational with three frontline squadrons and the Operational Conversion Unit, the aircraft carries Forward-Looking Infrared (FLIR) equipment which, when used in conjunction with the pilot's night vision goggles (NVGs), provides a night, low-altitude capability. The Harrier is also ideally suited to medium-level operations where it utilizes its highly accurate angle rate bombing system (ARBS), which employs a TV and laser dual mode tracker. The Harrier remains a highly versatile aircraft and can easily be deployed to remote forward operating locations. The Harrier T10, a two-seat trainer version of the GR7, came into service in 1995.

SPECIFICATIONS

Primary Role:	*ground-attack fighter*
Crew:	*1*
Contractor:	*BAe*
Length:	*14.36m (47.1ft)*
Wingspan:	*9.25m (30.3ft)*
Height:	*3.55m (11.6ft)*
Maximum Take-off Weight:	*14,061kg (31,000lb)*
Powerplant:	*1 x Pegasus Mk 105 turbofan*
Thrust:	*9773kg (21,500lb)*
Maximum Speed:	*1065km/h (661mph)*
Ceiling:	*15,000m (49,000ft)*
Range:	*2202km (1376 miles)*
Armament:	*2 x 25mm cannon, 16 Mk 82 or 6 Mk 83 bombs, BL-755 cluster bombs, Maverick ASM*
Systems:	*FLIR, ARBS, dual mode tracker (DMT)*
Date Deployed:	*1990*

HAWK

The Hawk is a light-attack and trainer aircraft which, through a continuing update and modernization programme, is still known as one of the world's best aircraft in its class. With a crew of two, it features low-mounted, swept-back wings that are tapered with curved tips. One turbofan engine is located inside the body, with semi-circular air intakes alongside the body forward of the wing roots and a single exhaust. The top line of the fuselage curves up from the pointed nose to incorporate the long, clear cockpit canopy, then slopes down to the jetpipe, giving a humped appearance, with slightly swept vertical and horizontal tail surfaces. The Royal Air Force (RAF) bought 175 Hawk Mk T1 aircraft in the late 1970s. RAF Hawks are used in advanced jet and weapons training. Other user countries include Brunei, Finland, Indonesia, Kenya, Kuwait, Malaysia, Oman, Saudi Arabia, South Korea and the United Arab Emirates. In the current RAF training programme, the Hawk T1 is used to teach operational tactics, air-to-air and air-to-ground firing, air combat and low-level operating procedures. To supplement the Tornado F3 force, some Hawk T1A advanced trainers have an additional task as point defence fighters. In this role they carry Sidewinder air-to-air missiles (AAMs) and a 30mm Aden cannon.

SPECIFICATIONS

Primary Role:	*trainer/ground-attack aircraft*
Crew:	*2*
Contractor:	*BAe*
Length:	*11.2m (36.6ft)*
Wingspan:	*9.39m (30.75ft)*
Height:	*3.9m (13ft)*
Maximum Take-off Weight:	*5700kg (12,566lb)*
Powerplant:	*1 x Rolls-Royce Turbomeca Adour turbofan*
Thrust:	*2591kg (5700lb)*
Maximum Speed:	*1010km/h (627mph)*
Ceiling:	*13,700m (44,947ft)*
Range:	*2917km (1823 miles)*
Armament:	*removable 30mm gun pod, five hardpoints; 3000kg (6614lb) warload, AIM-9 Sidewinder*
Systems:	*APG-66H, LINS 300*
Date Deployed:	*1976*

NIMROD MRA4

The Nimrod resembles the DH Comet, from which it derived: long "double bubble" fuselage with the cockpit built into the steeply raked nose. The fuselage tailcone extends well beyond the fin and rudder to house a magnetic anomaly detector (MAD) unit. An inflight refuelling probe projects from the fuselage above the cockpit. In July 1996 British Aerospace was selected as the prime contractor to supply a complete package of 21 mission-equipped Nimrod 2000 aircraft. A contract was awarded in December 1996, under which existing MR Mk 2 aircraft fuselage and empennage structures would be overhauled and reassembled, with redesigned wings and current-technology BR710 turbofan engines. The majority of the air vehicle systems have been replaced, including the flight deck, which will accommodate a reduced cockpit crew complement of two, facilitated by automated flight systems using modified Airbus A340 technology. The mission system, which is at the heart of the weapon system, is entirely new. The cabin interior is totally refitted to suit the new mission systems layout. This is therefore a new aircraft, not a refurbished one. In early 1998 the aircraft was renamed from Nimrod 2000 to Nimrod Maritime Reconnaissance and Attack Mk4 – Nimrod MRA4.

SPECIFICATIONS

Primary Role:	maritime reconnaissance
Crew:	13
Contractor:	BAe
Length:	38.63m (126.75ft)
Wingspan:	35m (114.9ft)
Height:	9m (29.6ft)
Maximum Take-off Weight:	80,510kg (177,500lb)
Powerplant:	4 x RB168-20 250 turbofans
Thrust:	5518kg (12,140lb) each
Maximum Speed:	926km/h (575mph)
Ceiling:	12,800m (41,994ft)
Range:	8340km (5212 miles)
Armament:	torpedoes, bombs and depth charges, Sidewinder AAMs
Systems:	tactical command system, armament control system, 2000MR radar, ESM, FLIR, MAD
Date Deployed:	2005

NIMROD MR2

The Nimrod MR2 is a maritime patrol aircraft used for maritime surface surveillance and anti-submarine warfare. Carrying a crew of 13, the aircraft is fitted with radar and magnetic and acoustic detection equipment. The Nimrod maritime patrol aircraft can also assist in search and rescue operations by searching for survivors, giving guidance to rescue craft at the scene, and dropping survival equipment if needed. Equipment includes an advanced search radar, offering greater range and sensitivity coupled with a higher data processing rate; a new acoustic processing system which is compatible with a wide range of existing and projected sonobuoys; and early warning support measures (EWSM) equipment in a pod at each wingtip. Aircraft deployed to Ascension Island during the 1982 Falklands campaign were fitted with Sidewinder air-to-air missiles (AAMs) for self-defence. Air-to-air refuelling probes were fitted at that time to 16 aircraft (redesignated MR Mk 2P), making possible flights of up to 19 hours. Ample space and power is available in the basic Nimrod design to accept additional or alternative sensors such as sideways-looking infrared linescan, low-light level TV and digital processing of intercepted signals. The MR2 fleet will be replaced by Nimrod MRA4 in a refurbishment programme.

SPECIFICATIONS

Primary Role:	anti-submarine patrol aircraft
Crew:	13
Contractor:	BAe
Length:	38.63m (126.75ft)
Wingspan:	35m (114.9ft)
Height:	9m (29.6ft)
Maximum Take-off Weight:	80,510kg (177,500lb)
Powerplant:	4 x RB168-20 250 turbojets
Thrust:	5518kg (12,140lb) each
Maximum Speed:	926km/h (575mph)
Ceiling:	12,800m (41,994ft)
Range:	8340km (5212 miles)
Armament:	Sidewinder AAMs, Harpoon ASMs, torpedoes
Systems:	EWSM, Replacement Acoustic Processor, Searchwater radar
Date Deployed:	1979

NIMROD R1

Originally designed as a maritime patrol and anti-submarine aircraft, the Nimrod is less well known for its secondary role. The original maritime equipment was removed from the airframe, and replaced with a highly sophisticated and sensitive suite of systems used for reconnaissance and the gathering of electronic intelligence. The ability of the Nimrod to loiter for long periods, following a high-speed dash to the required area of operation, make the aircraft ideally suited to this task. The Nimrod R1s are externally distinguishable from the maritime reconnaissance version by the absence of the magnetic anomaly detection tail booms and a distinctive pod on the leading edge of the port wing. Inflight refuelling probes were added in 1982. There is a powerful searchlight on the starboard wing, mounted on a fuel tank called the 4A tank. The searchlight is seven-million candle power and cannot be struck on the ground for more than a few seconds or the heat generated destroys the searchlight. The Nimrod R1 has four Rolls-Royce Spey 250 series twin spool bypass jet engines giving 5518kg (12,140lb) of thrust each. Maximum speed is 926km/h (575mph) and cruise speed is just below 800km/h (500mph). Mission endurance is around eight hours without aerial tanking.

SPECIFICATIONS

Primary Role:	*electronic inteliigence gathering*
Crew:	*12*
Contractor:	*BAe*
Length:	*38.63m (126.75ft)*
Wingspan:	*35m (114.9ft)*
Height:	*9m (29.6ft)*
Maximum Take-off Weight:	*80,000kg (176,000lb)*
Powerplant:	*4 x Rolls-Royce RB168-20 Spey 250 turbofans*
Thrust:	*5518kg (12,140lb) each*
Maximum Speed:	*926km/h (575mph)*
Ceiling:	*12,800m (41,994ft)*
Range:	*8340km (5212 miles)*
Armament:	*none*
Systems:	*Ferranti 1600D computer, Loral electronic support measures (ESM) pods*
Date Deployed:	*1969*

SEA HARRIER

The Sea Harrier is optimized for air-to-air combat with secondary missions of surveillance, air-to-sea and air-to-ground attack. The FA2 is the latest version in service with the Royal Navy (45 aircraft). The aircraft is able to detect and destroy threats before the launch of an attack using long-range weapon systems with look-down and shoot-down tactical capability. A Smiths Industries weapon stores management system ensures the correct selection and release of weapons. The aircraft has five weapons stations. Weapons are mounted on launchers: Raytheon LAU-106A ejection-launchers and Varo LAU-7 rail launchers. The FA2 is equipped with the Raytheon AIM-120A advanced medium-range air-to-air missile (AMRAAM), which is an all-weather, fire-and-forget missile equipped with an active radar seeker and range of over 80km (50 miles). The AIM-9 Sidewinder air-to-air missile (AAM) provides the Harrier with capability for firing at close range at an approaching enemy aircraft in a dogfight. The Sea Harrier's anti-ship missile is the Sea Eagle, a fire-and-forget sea-skimming missile with active radar homing and a range of over 80km (50 miles). It can carry the ALARM anti-radiation missile, which can be deployed in direct attack mode against a radar target or in loiter mode, where the missile waits for the hostile radar to emit.

SPECIFICATIONS

Primary Role:	carrier-borne multirole fighter
Crew:	1
Contractor:	BAe
Length:	14.17m (46.5ft)
Wingspan:	7.70m (25.25ft)
Height:	3.71m (12.1ft)
Maximum Take-off Weight:	11,880kg (26,136lb)
Powerplant:	1 x Rolls-Royce Pegasus turbofan
Thrust:	9773kg (21,500lb)
Maximum Speed:	1200mph (750 miles)
Ceiling:	15,240m (50,000ft)
Range:	1500km (937 miles)
Armament:	2 x 30mm cannon, AMRAAM, AIM-7M AAMs, Sea Eagle ASM, ALARM
Systems:	pulse Doppler radar, TACAN, IPG-100F GPS
Date Deployed:	1993

TRISTAR

The RAF operates a number of Tristar aircraft in the transport role. The Tristar C2s are dedicated transport aircraft and can carry 265 passengers and 16 tonnes (35,000lb) of freight over ranges in excess of 6400km (4000 miles). The other two variants, the K1 and the KC1, are dual role and capable of providing air-to-air refuelling from a pair of centerline fuselage hoses. The K1 can carry 204 passengers; however, the KC1 has a large freight door and can carry 20 cargo pallets, 196 passengers or a combination of mixed freight and passengers. The VC10 and Tristar fleets are based at RAF Brize Norton in Oxfordshire, England. Powerplants consist of two engines in underwing nacelles and one engine mounted on top of the fuselage forward of the swept fin, with the jet efflux below the rudder through the tail cone. The Tristar has a circular, wide-body fuselage with low-set wings at the midway point, and swept tailplane low set either side of the rear fuselage below the fin. Refuelling pods are located under the wings. The KC1 aerial tanker variant has a large portside cargo door and tanks installed under the cabin floor to carry a total capacity of 13,636kg (30,000lb) of fuel. It has twin hose and drogue units in the rear fuselage and an inflight refuelling probe. When not a tanker it can also carry passengers.

SPECIFICATIONS

Primary Role:	transport/tanker
Crew:	4
Contractor:	Lockheed Martin
Length:	50.09m (164.3ft)
Wingspan:	50.17m (164.6ft)
Height:	16.87m (55.3ft)
Maximum Take-off Weight:	224,980kg (496,000lb)
Powerplant:	3 x Rolls-Royce RB211-524B4 turbofans
Thrust:	22,727kg (50,000lb) each
Maximum Speed:	964km/h (602mph)
Ceiling:	13,105m (42,995ft)
Range:	7783km (4864 miles)
Armament:	none
Systems:	Collins flight control system, Sperry air data computer
Date Deployed:	1985

KFIR

The Kfir (which means lion cub) is basically a redesigned Mirage 5 with a canard mounted on the air intake. The wings are low-mounted, delta-shaped with a sawtooth in the leading edges. There are small canards mounted on the air intakes with one turbojet engine inside the fuselage. There are semi-circular air intakes alongside the fuselage, with a large, single exhaust. The fuselage is tube-shaped with a long, solid, pointed nose. The body widens at the air intakes. There is a bubble canopy flush with the spine. The tail has no tail flats. The fin is swept-back and tapered with a prominent step in the leading edge. The Kfir-C7, the definitive single-seat version introduced in 1983, is based on the Kfir-C2 with a specially adapted version of the J79-GEJ1E engine with some 454kg (1000lb) more afterburning thrust. This type has two extra hardpoints and a number of advanced features including capability for the carriage and use of "smart" weapons, Elta EL/M-2021B pulse doppler radar, a revised cockpit with more sophisticated electronics and hands on throttle and stick (HOTAS) controls, and provision for inflight refueling. Maximum take-off weight is increased by 1540kg (3395lb), but combat radius and (more importantly) thrust-to-weight ratio are improved to a marked degree.

SPECIFICATIONS

Primary Role:	multirole fighter
Crew:	1
Contractor:	Israel Aircraft Industries
Length:	15.65m (51.3ft)
Wingspan:	8.22m (26.96ft)
Height:	4.55m (14.9ft)
Maximum Take-off Weight:	16,500kg (36,300lb)
Powerplant:	1 x J79-J1E turbojet
Thrust:	5405kg (11,890lb)
Maximum Speed:	2426km/h (1516mph)
Ceiling:	unknown
Range:	776km (485 miles)
Armament:	2 x 30mm cannon, Magic 550 AIM-9, Shafrir or Python AAMs
Systems:	Elta EL/M-2021B pulse doppler radar, HOTAS (hands on throttle and stick) controls
Date Deployed:	1973

F-2

The F-2 is the replacement for Japan's ageing, domestic F-1 fighter. The cooperatively developed and produced Japanese F-2 single-engine fighter (FS-X) has performance capabilities roughly comparable to those of the US F-16, but costs over three times as much and about the same as the larger two-engine F-15. The F-2 Support Fighter is a multirole, single-engine fighter aircraft produced for the Japan Air Self Defense Force. It was co-developed and is now being co-produced by Mitsubishi Heavy Industries (MHI) of Japan and Lockheed Martin Aeronautics Company (principal US subcontractor to MHI). Based on the design of the Lockheed Martin Aeronautics Company F-16C/D Fighting Falcon, the F-2 is customized to the unique requirements of the Japan Defense Agency. Although capable of both air-to-air and air-to-surface roles, the F-2 emphasizes the air-to-surface role because its primary mission is sea lane protection. The F-2 has a wing area enlarged approximately 25 percent compared to the F-16's wing, allowing more internal fuel storage and two more weapon store stations. The wing is made from graphite epoxy using state-of-the-art composite technology to maximize strength while minimizing weight. In addition to the larger wing area, the F-2 fuselage has also been enlarged by 406mm (16in).

SPECIFICATIONS

Primary Role:	*multirole fighter*
Crew:	*1*
Contractor:	*Mitsubishi, Lockheed Martin*
Length:	*15.52m (50.9ft)*
Wingspan:	*10.8m (35.4ft)*
Height:	*4.96m (16.2ft)*
Maximum Take-off Weight:	*22,272kg (49,000lb)*
Powerplant:	*1 x GE F110-129 turbofan*
Thrust:	*unknown*
Maximum Speed:	*2125km/h (1320mph)*
Ceiling:	*unknown*
Range:	*833km (521 miles)*
Armament:	*1 x 20mm gun, Sparrow & Sidewinder AAMs, ASM-1 & ASM-2 anti-ship missiles*
Systems:	*active phased-array, multi-function display (MFD), HUD*
Date Deployed:	*2000*

A-50 MAINSTAY

The A-50 Mainstay is based on a stretched Ilyushin Il-76 transport combined with an upgraded "Flat Jack" radar system. Developed to replace the Tu-126 Moss (a variant of the Bear bomber), the Mainstay first flew in 1980 with about 40 produced by 1992. The Mainstay is not as sophisticated as its Western counterpart, the E-3 Sentry, but provides Russian fighter regiments with an airborne control capability over both land and water. Mainstays have been used by the Russian Air Force at bases in the Kola Peninsula and for observing Allied air operations during the 1991 Gulf War. In 1994 NATO proposed making the E-3 Sentry and the Mainstay interoperable to enable Russia to provide AEW&C support to future United Nations or coalition operations. The aircraft's wings are high-mounted, swept-back, and tapered with blunt tips. There are four turbofan engines mounted on pylons under and extending beyond the wings' leading edges. The fuselage is long, round and tapered to the rear with a radome on the chin. There is a saucer type radome on top of the aircraft. The aircraft can stay aloft without refueling for four to six hours and can remain airborne for another four hours with mid-air refueling. The radar has a detection range of up to 800km (500 miles) and can track 200 targets simultaneously.

SPECIFICATIONS

Primary Role:	airborne early warning
Crew:	15
Contractor:	Ilyushin/Beriev
Length:	46.59m (152.9ft)
Wingspan:	50.5m (165.6ft)
Height:	14.76m (48.5ft)
Maximum Take-off Weight:	190,000kg (418,000lb)
Powerplant:	4 x D-30KP turbofans
Thrust:	12,025kg (26,455lb) each
Maximum Speed:	850km/h (528mph)
Ceiling:	10,200m (33,465ft)
Range:	7300km (4536 miles)
Armament:	wingtip ECM pods and self-defence flares
Systems:	Schnel-M airborne radar and guidance system, NPK-T flight control and navigation system
Date Deployed:	1984

AN-70

Without the break-up of the former Soviet Union, the An-70, which was designed to meet the needs of the air force's transport needs, would probably be already in service today. However, the programme got caught up in the chaos generated by the political changes in Russia which propelled the formerly centrally controlled aerospace industry into a serious crisis. The An-70 heavy transport is a replacement for the An-12 "Cub". The first flight was on 16 December 1994. It has the same high wing and tail loading ramp that are typical among tactical freight aircraft, but a novelty is the use of contra-rotating propfans (with six and eight blades). The landing gear permits the An-70 to operate from unpaved airfields, and expected airframe life is 20,000 flights (45,000 flight hours, 25 years' service). The aircraft is equipped with a highly computerized control system, allowing quick diagnostics and service. The navigator's position is eliminated, with his functions and equipment transferred to the first officer's station. The flight engineer and radio operator stations are also eliminated. The pressurized cargo cabin has a temperature regulator and is equipped with in-floor cargo handling system, which makes the An-70 a self-sufficient aircraft that has no need for ground handling equipment. Production estimates are unknown.

SPECIFICATIONS

Primary Role:	transport
Crew:	3
Contractor:	Antonov
Length:	40.25m (132ft)
Wingspan:	44.06m (144.5ft)
Height:	16.1m (52.8ft)
Maximum Take-off Weight:	130,000kg (286,000lb)
Powerplant:	4 x ZMKB Ivchenko Progress D-27 propfans
Thrust:	unknown
Maximum Speed:	750km/h (469mph)
Ceiling:	9600m (31,496ft)
Range:	7250km (4531 miles)
Armament:	none
Systems:	unknown
Date Deployed:	unknown

AN-72 COALER

The An-72 Coaler is designed as a short take-off and landing (STOL) aircraft which can operate from unprepared airfields. The first prototype flew on 22 December 1977. The wings are high-mounted and back-tapered, with two turbofans mounted in long pods mounted on top of the wings. Round air intakes extend from the front of the wings' leading edges. The engines were placed on the leading edge of the wings to increase lift for STOL capability, with the jet exhausts blowing over titanium panels on the upper surface. The fuselage is circular with a round, solid nose, upswept rear section and a flush cockpit. The rear fuselage has a hinged loading ramp with a rear fairing that slides backwards and up to clear the opening. Loads can be air dropped, and there are folding side seats for 42 para-troops or 52 passengers. The An-72P is a maritime patrol variant with bulged observation windows, life raft provision and cameras as well as offensive armament, including under-wing rocket pods, a podded cannon on the undercarriage sponson and bombs that can be mounted in the rear fuselage and dropped through the open rear ramp. The An-74 derivative features improved avionics, radar and increased range. It was designed to operate in the polar regions where it can land on ice floes for re-supply or rescue work.

SPECIFICATIONS

Primary Role:	*light STOL transport*
Crew:	*3*
Contractor:	*Antonov*
Length:	*28.1m (92ft)*
Wingspan:	*31.9m (104.5ft)*
Height:	*8.6m (28.3ft)*
Maximum Take-off Weight:	*34,500kg (76,060lb)*
Powerplant:	*2 x ZKMB Progress D-36 turbofans*
Thrust:	*13,027kg (28,660lb) each*
Maximum Speed:	*705km/h (438mph)*
Ceiling:	*11,800m (38,713ft)*
Range:	*4800km (3000 miles)*
Armament:	*none*
Systems:	*integrated flight control system*
Date Deployed:	*1979*

AN-124 CONDOR

The An-124 *Ruslan* is the world's largest and highest flying cargo capacity aircraft in production. The aircraft, which has the NATO reporting name Condor, is designed for long-range delivery and air dropping of heavy and large-size cargo, including machines, equipment and troops. The unique transport capabilities and high performance of the aircraft have been proven in operation. Examples include 91-tonne (90-ton) hydraulic turbines, large-size Liebherr autocranes, American Euclid dump trucks, the fuselage of a Tu-204 passenger transporter, a 111-tonne (109-ton) railway locomotive, and a sea yacht of more than 25m (82ft) in length. The aircraft fuselage has a double-deck layout. The cockpit, the relief crew compartment and the troop cabin with 88 seats are on the upper deck. The lower deck is the cargo hold. The flight deck has crew stations arranged in pairs for the six crew members: pilot and co-pilot, two flight engineers, the navigator and communications officer. The loadmaster's station is located in the lobby deck. The An-124 has a swept-back supercritical wing to give high aerodynamic efficiency and consequently a long flight range. The construction includes extruded skin panels on the wing, extruded plates for the centre-section wing panels and monolithic wafer plates for the fuselage panels.

SPECIFICATIONS

Primary Role:	*heavy transport*
Crew:	*6*
Contractor:	*Antonov*
Length:	*69.1m (226.6ft)*
Wingspan:	*73.3m (240.6ft)*
Height:	*20.8m (68.1ft)*
Maximum Take-off Weight:	*405,000kg (891,000lb)*
Powerplant:	*4 x Lotarev D18T turbofans*
Thrust:	*23,477kg (51,650lb) each*
Maximum Speed:	*865km/h (537mph)*
Ceiling:	*12,000m (39,370ft)*
Range:	*13,300km (8312 miles)*
Armament:	*none*
Systems:	*integrated flight control and aiming-navigation system*
Date Deployed:	*1984*

IL-76 CANDID

The Il-76 is a medium-range military transport aircraft known by the NATO codename Candid. The mission of the aircraft is to drop paratroopers; carry ground forces; combat materials with crews and armaments including medium-sized battle tanks; and also transport materials for disaster relief operations. The Il-76 is produced by the Ilyushin Aviation Company in Moscow and the Tashkent Aircraft Production Corporation in Tashkent, Uzbekistan. There are several design variants including the basic Il-76, Il-76M, Il-76MD and the Il-76-MF. In terms of design, aerodynamic configuration and flight performance characteristics, the Il-76M version virtually resembles the basic Il-76 aircraft, but has almost double the payload capacity. The aircraft is of a conventional aerodynamic configuration with a high-set swept wing and T-shaped tail unit. The crew cabin, cargo hold and rear compartment are fully pressurized. The beam-type fuselage has an oval section over the crew cabin and circular section over the cargo hold. The wing leading and trailing edges are fitted with highlift devices comprising deflectable five-section leading-edge slats, triple-slotted trailing-edge extension flaps, ailerons, spoilers and air brakes. The Il-76 is the true workhorse of the Russian aviation transport fleet.

SPECIFICATIONS

Primary Role:	*medium transport*
Crew:	*6*
Contractor:	*Ilyushin*
Length:	*46.6m (152.8ft)*
Wingspan:	*50.5m (165.6ft)*
Height:	*14.7m (48.22ft)*
Maximum Take-off Weight:	*170,000kg (374,000lb)*
Powerplant:	*4 x Soloviev D-30KP turbofans*
Thrust:	*12,025kg (26,455lb) each*
Maximum Speed:	*850km/h (528mph)*
Ceiling:	*10,500m (34,448ft)*
Range:	*7300km (4562 miles)*
Armament:	*2 x 23mm GSh-23L cannons in the tail*
Systems:	*integrated flight control and aiming-navigation system*
Date Deployed:	*1974*

IL-78 MIDAS

The Il-78 Midas aerial refuelling tanker is based on (or converted from) the airframe of the Il-76MD freighter, carrying a maximum payload of 48,000kg (105,600lb). When deployed in the early 1980s, it supported tactical and strategic aircraft and significantly improved the ability of Soviet aircraft to conduct longer-range operations. The former Soviet Union's only operational Il-78M regiment was based in the Ukraine, which retained the aircraft after independence. Only a handful remained in Russian hands. A three-point UPAZ-1A Sakhalin refuelling system allows it to serve one heavy bomber from the ventral point or two aircraft (MiG-31 or Su-24) simultaneously from the wing-mount points. The refuelling process is monitored by an operator occupying the gunner's position. His workplace is equipped with an optical rear view system, in addition to a radio and light signal equipment. Once connected, refuelled aircraft can receive fuel from the wing tanks at rate 900 to 2200 litres per minute. While early production Il-78s had removable fuselage tanks and could be used as military transports, the later, improved version Il-78M cannot be converted to a transporter. Midas entered service in 1987, replacing the outdated M-4 tankers that had served since the 1960s.

SPECIFICATIONS

Primary Role:	airborne tanker
Crew:	6
Contractor:	Ilyushin
Length:	46.6m (152.8ft)
Wingspan:	50.5m (165.6ft)
Height:	14.7m (48.4ft)
Maximum Take-off Weight:	210,000kg (462,000lb)
Powerplant:	4 x Soloviev D-30KP turbofans
Thrust:	12,025kg (26,455lb) each
Maximum Speed:	850km/h (528mph)
Ceiling:	10,500m (34,448ft)
Range:	2500km (1562 miles)
Armament:	2 x 23mm GSh-23L cannons in the tail
Systems:	integrated flight control and aiming-navigation system
Date Deployed:	1987

MIG-29 FULCRUM

The mission of the MiG-29 is to destroy hostile air targets within radar coverage limits and also to destroy ground targets using unguided weapons in visual flight conditions. The aircraft's fixed-wing profile with large-wing leading-edge root extensions gives good manoeuvrability and control at subsonic speed, including manoeuvres at high angles of attack. It is equipped with seven external weapon hardpoints. The aircraft can carry up to two R-27 air-to-air medium-range missiles; six R-73 and R-60 air-to-air short-range missiles; four pods of S-5, S-8 and S-24 unguided rockets; air bombs weighing up to 3000kg (6600lb); and a 30mm built-in aircraft gun with 150 rounds of ammunition. The aircraft is equipped with an information and fire control radar system comprising an N-019 radar developed by Phazotron Research and Production Company, Moscow; an infrared search and track sensor; a laser rangefinder; and a helmet-mounted target designator. The Russian Air Force has begun an upgrade programme for 150 of its MiG-29 fighters, which will be designated MiG-29SMT. The upgrade comprises increased range and payload, new glass cockpit, new avionics, improved radar, and an inflight refuelling probe. The radar will be the Phazotron Zhuk, capable of tracking 10 targets to a maximum range of 245km (153 miles).

SPECIFICATIONS

Primary Role:	*fighter*
Crew:	*1*
Contractor:	*Moscow Air Production Organization*
Length:	*14.87m (48.75ft)*
Wingspan:	*11.36m (37.25ft)*
Height:	*4.73m (15.5ft)*
Maximum Take-off Weight:	*18,500kg (40,785lb)*
Powerplant:	*2 x RD-33 turbofans*
Thrust:	*8300kg (18,260lb) each*
Maximum Speed:	*2400km/hr (1500mph)*
Ceiling:	*18,000m (59,055ft)*
Range:	*1500km (937 miles)*
Armament:	*AA-10, AA-11 & AA-8 AAMs, 1 x 30mm gun, bombs*
Systems:	*Slot Back radar, IRST, RWR, ballistic bombsight*
Date Deployed:	*1983*

SU-24 FENCER

The Su-24 Fencer is designed to penetrate hostile territory and destroy ground and surface targets in any weather conditions, by day and night. Variants of the Su-24 have also been produced for reconnaissance and electronic countermeasures duties. The aircraft has a conventional aerodynamic configuration with a variable-sweep shoulder wing. The fuselage is of rectangular section semi-monocoque design with a two-seat pressurized cockpit. The wing sweep-back angle varies from 16 to 69 degrees with respect to the wing leading edge. The tail unit comprises all-moving horizontal tail surfaces and a single-fin vertical tail fitted with a rudder. The horizontal tail surfaces function as elevators when deflecting symmetrically and as ailerons when deflecting differentially, and a tricycle-type landing gear allows the aircraft to be operated from either concrete or unpaved runways. The Su-24M entered service in 1983 and is a development of the Su-24. Over 900 Su-24s have been delivered and the aircraft is in service with the Russian Air Force and Navy and the air forces of Azerbaijan, Algeria, Iran, Libya, Poland, Syria and the Ukraine. As well as bombs and missiles, the aircraft can carry up to three gun pods with 23mm Gsh-6-23 guns, which have a rate of fire of 9000 rounds per minute and fire unit of 500 rounds.

SPECIFICATIONS

Primary Role:	tactical bomber
Crew:	2
Contractor:	Sukhoi
Length:	24.53m (80.5ft)
Wingspan:	17.63m (57.8ft) to10.36m (34ft)
Height:	4.97m (16.25ft)
Maximum Take-off Weight:	39,700kg (87,520lb)
Powerplant:	2 x AL-21F-3A turbojets
Thrust:	22,454kg (49,400lb) each
Maximum Speed:	1550km/hr (969mph)
Ceiling:	11,000m (36,089ft)
Range:	2100km (1312 miles)
Armament:	1 x 23mm six-barrelled cannon, AS-7, AS-10, AS-11, AS-12, AS-13, AS-14 AGMs
Systems:	PNS-24 integrated navigation and aiming system
Date Deployed:	1983

SU-25 FROGFOOT

The Su-25 is designed to defeat small mobile and stationary ground targets and to engage low-speed air targets. A two-seat variant, the Su-35UB (Frogfoot-B), is a weapons training aircraft manufactured at Ulan-Ude. The Su-25UTG is the two-seater aircraft carrier variant fitted with an arrester hook under the tail. The Su-25UTG is deployed on the Russian Navy aircraft carrier *Admiral Kuznetsov*. An upgraded Su-25K, the Scorpion, has been developed by Tbilisi Aerospace Manufacturing (TAM) of Georgia with Elbit of Israel. Scorpion has a new advanced avionics system with a weapons delivery and navigation system for both NATO and Eastern European weapons and pods, and new glass cockpit with two multi-colour LCD displays and head-up display (HUD). The aircraft's twin-barrel gun, the 30mm AO-17A, is installed in the underside of the fuselage on the port side. The gun is armed with 250 rounds of ammunition and is capable of firing at a burst rate of 3000 rounds per minute. SPPU-22 gun pods can also be installed on the underwing pylons. The pods carry the GSh-23 23mm twin-barrel guns, each with 260 rounds of ammunition. The aircraft is equipped with self-sealing foam-filled fuel tanks, and its range can be extended by the provision of four PTB-1500 external fuel tanks.

SPECIFICATIONS

Primary Role:	*close support*
Crew:	*1*
Contractor:	*Sukhoi*
Length:	*15.53m (50.9ft)*
Wingspan:	*14.36m (47ft)*
Height:	*4.8m (15.75ft)*
Maximum Take-off Weight:	*17,600kg (38,800lb)*
Powerplant:	*2 x R-195 turbojets*
Thrust:	*9019kg (19,842lb) each*
Maximum Speed:	*975km/h (606mph)*
Ceiling:	*7000m (22,966ft)*
Range:	*1250km (781 miles)*
Armament:	*1 x twin 30mm cannon, AA-8, AA-10 AAMs; AS-7, AS-10, AS-14 AGMs*
Systems:	*Klyon PS target designator, Gardeniya radar jammer*
Date Deployed:	*1981*

SU-27 FLANKER

Designed as a high-performance fighter with a fly-by-wire control system, the highly manoeuvrable Su-27 is one of the most imposing fighters ever built. The first "Flanker-A'" prototype flew on 20 May 1977 and entered service as the "Flanker-B" in 1984. The development of the Su-27 fighter was completed in the early 1980s, and the aircraft subsequently set more than 40 world records of altitude and take-off speed. It was the forerunner of an entire family of fighter aircraft, including the Su-27UB training variant, the Su-33 carrier-based fighter, the Su-37 multi-mission aircraft and the Su-32FN two-seat specialized version. The Su-27UB is a two-seat training version of the Su-27 which first flew in March 1985. The aircraft is equipped to operate autonomously in combat over hostile territory, as an escort to deep-penetration strike aircraft, and in the suppression of enemy airfields. The Flanker also provides general air defence in cooperation with ground and airborne control stations. The Su-27 is in service with Russia, Ukraine, Belarus, Kazakhstan and Vietnam, and is built under licence in China, where it is designated the F-11. A variant, the Su-30MK, has also been sold to India where licensed local production began in 2000. There is no doubt that Flanker is one of the most potent warplanes in service.

SPECIFICATIONS

Primary Role:	*interceptor*
Crew:	*1*
Contractor:	*Sukhoi*
Length:	*21.935m (71.9ft)*
Wingspan:	*14.7m (48.2ft)*
Height:	*5.932m (19.5ft)*
Maximum Take-off Weight:	*22,000kg (48,400lb)*
Powerplant:	*2 x Lyulka AL-31F turbofans*
Thrust:	*25,052kg (55,114lb) each*
Maximum Speed:	*2500km/h (1562mph)*
Ceiling:	*18,500m (60695ft)*
Range:	*4000km (2500 miles)*
Armament:	*1 x 30mm cannon, AA-8, AA-9, AA-10, AA-11, AAMs*
Systems:	*Pulse Doppler radar, fly-by-wire system*
Date Deployed:	*1984*

SU-27P FLANKER

Largely based on the Su-27UB two-seat trainer, the Su-27P has a new radio location system which can transmit the positions of 10 targets to four other fighters at the same time. The Su-27P (also called the Su-30) is made at Irkutsk. Due to development difficulties, work on the two-seat version had to be set aside until the single-seat version was in production, and the first two-seat T10U prototype did not fly until March 1985, entering production and service as the Sukhoi Su-27UB two years later. The Su-27UB has a tandem-seat arrangement under a single canopy, with the back seat stepped up above the front seat, providing the flight instructor in the back seat a good view in front of the aircraft and of what the trainee in the front seat is doing. This arrangement gives the Su-27UB an even more "crane-necked" appearance than the Su-27. The Su-27UB was designed to be fully combat capable, and the second seat was accommodated by stretching the fuselage. The vertical tail-fins were increased in height slightly to compensate for the changed aerodynamics. The addition of the second seat increased the weight of the aircraft by only about 1120kg (2470lb) without reduction in fuel capacity, and aside from minor decreases in top speed, the Su-27P's performance is very similar to that of the single-seat Su-27.

SPECIFICATIONS

Primary Role:	*long-range intercept fighter*
Crew:	*2*
Contractor:	*Sukhoi*
Length:	*21.94m (71.98ft)*
Wingspan:	*14.70m (48.22ft)*
Height:	*6.36m (20.86ft)*
Maximum Take-off Weight:	*34,000kg (74,800lb)*
Powerplant:	*2 x Lyulka AL-31 turbofans*
Thrust:	*25,051kg (55,114lb) each*
Maximum Speed:	*2125km/h (1328mph)*
Ceiling:	*17,500m (57,414ft)*
Range:	*5200km (3250 miles)*
Armament:	*1 x 30mm gun, AA-10, AA-11, AA-12 AAMs, bombs*
Systems:	*Phazotron N001 Zhuk pulse Doppler radar, OEPS-27 electro-optic system, fly-by-wire system*
Date Deployed:	*1987*

TU-95 BEAR

Development of the Tu-95 Bear bomber began in the early 1950s after series production of the medium-range Tu-4 started. The Bear's wings are mid-mounted, swept-back and tapered with blunt tips, and the engine nacelles extend well beyond the wings' leading edges. The fuselage of the Bear is tube-shaped with a rounded nose that tapers to the rear. It also has a stepped cockpit and a tail gun compartment. The tail of the aircraft is a fin that is swept-back and tapered with a square tip. There have been many variants, the most modern being the Bear H, the Tu-95MS. This entirely new variant became the launch platform for the long-range Kh-55 (AS-15) air-launched cruise missile. The initial version carried the missiles located in the bomb bay on a catapult. This was the first new production of a strike version of the Bear airframe since the 1960s. With the Bear H in series production, the decline in the inventory of Bear aircraft was reversed. The version designated as Tu-95MS6 aircraft carried Kh-55s located in the bomb bay on a rotary launcher. The Tu-95MS16 carried six missiles inside the fuselage and 10 missiles underneath the wings. Three underwing pylons are fitted under each inner wing panel. The Bear will remain in service until 2015, Russia's fragile finances permitting.

SPECIFICATIONS

Primary Role:	strategic bomber
Crew:	7
Contractor:	Tupolev
Length:	49.6m (162.7ft)
Wingspan:	51.1m (167.6ft)
Height:	13.4m (44ft)
Maximum Take-off Weight:	185,000kg (407,000lb)
Powerplant:	4 x NK-12MV turboprops
Thrust:	6818kg (15,000lb) each
Maximum Speed:	830km/h (519mph)
Ceiling:	12,000m (39,370ft)
Range:	10,500km (6562 miles)
Armament:	2 x 23mm guns, 16 x Kh-55
Systems:	Clam Pipe nav/bombing radar, Box Tail gun fire control radar, ECM, Ground Bouncer ECM jamming system, RWR
Date Deployed:	1981 (Bear H)

TU-160 BLACKJACK

The Tu-160 is a multi-mission strategic bomber designed for operations ranging from subsonic speeds and low altitudes to speeds over Mach 1 at high altitudes. The two weapons bays can accommodate different mission-specific loads, including strategic cruise missiles, short-range guided missiles, nuclear and conventional bombs, and mines. Its basic armament of short-range guided missiles and strategic cruise missiles enables it to deliver nuclear strikes against targets with pre-assigned coordinates. The Tu-160 was the outcome of a multi-mission bomber competition, which included a Tupolev proposal for an aircraft design using elements of the Tu-144, the Myasishchev M-18, and a Sukhoi design based on the T-4 aircraft. The project of Myasishchev was considered to be the most successful, although the Tupolev organization was regarded as having the greatest potential for completing this complex project. Consequently, Tupolev was assigned to develop an aircraft using elements of the Myasishchev M-18 bomber design. The project was supervised by V.N. Binznyuk. Trial operations in the air force began in 1987 with serial production being conducted at the Kazan Aviation Association. The Blackjack programme has encountered severe financial problems, and its future is uncertain.

SPECIFICATIONS

Primary Role:	strategic bomber
Crew:	4
Contractor:	Tupolev
Length:	54.1m (177.5ft)
Wingspan:	55.7m (182.75ft) to 50.7m (166.3ft)
Height:	13.1m (43ft)
Maximum Take-off Weight:	275,000kg (606,260lb)
Powerplant:	4 x MK-321 turbofans
Thrust:	25,000kg (55,000lb) each
Maximum Speed:	2000km/h (1250mph)
Ceiling:	16,000m (52,493ft)
Range:	12,300km (7687 miles)
Armament:	12 AS-16 SRAMs, 6 Kh-55 cruise missiles, nuclear weapons
Systems:	RID combined navigation-and-weapon aiming system, radio-electronic warfare systems
Date Deployed:	1987

YAK-141 FREESTYLE

The Yak-141 (formerly Yak-41) was originally intended to replace the Yak-38 for air defence of Kiev class carriers/cruisers, with secondary attack capabilities. Designed for carrier-borne operations as an air interceptor, close air combat, maritime and ground-attack, the Yak-141 has the same multi-mode radar as the MiG-29, although with a slightly smaller antenna housed in the nose radome. It features a triplex full authority digital fly-by-wire system. The Yak-141 continues previous Soviet V/STOL principles: combining a lift and propulsion jet with two fuselage-mounted lift jets in tandem behind the cockpit, with cruise power provided by a single Tumansky R-79 jet engine. The R-79 has a rear lift/cruise nozzle which deflects down for take-off, while the two lift engines have corresponding rearward vector to ensure stability. The airframe makes extensive use of composite materials, with some 28 percent of the airframe constructed of carbon-fibre, primarily in the tail assembly, while the remainder of the structure is mainly aluminum lithium alloys. The project began in 1975, but was delayed by financial constraints as well as the protracted development of the engine, which meant the prototype did not fly until March 1989. Four prototypes were built, two continuing in flight testing until 1995.

SPECIFICATIONS

Primary Role:	air defence
Crew:	1
Contractor:	Yakovlev
Length:	18.36m (60.2ft)
Wingspan:	10.105m (33.1ft) to 5.9m (19.3ft)
Height:	5m (16.3ft)
Maximum Take-off Weight:	19,500kg (42,900lb)
Powerplant:	1 x R-79-300 turbofan, 2 x Rybinsk RD-41 turbofans
Thrust:	15,500kg (34,100lb)
Maximum Speed:	1250km/hr (781mph)
Ceiling:	15,000m (49,000ft)
Range:	2100km (1312 miles)
Armament:	1 x 30mm cannon, AA-10 AAMs, bombs, rockets
Systems:	multi-mode radar, HUD, OR-69 Sirena 3 RWR, ECM systems
Date Deployed:	unknown

C-212 AVIOCAR

The C-212 Aviocar 100 has a metal structure with a fixed tricycle landing gear and propellers with a variable and reversible pitch. Being a short take-off and landing (STOL) aircraft, it can use short runways. The C-212 is CASA's answer to the needs of different air forces in the field of light military transport and can operate in areas lacking in infrastructure and from unpaved runways. The C-212 was designed with simple and reliable systems. The wings are high-mounted and unequally tapered from mid-wing to the square tips. Two turboprop engines are mounted in pods under the wings' leading edges. The thick, cigar-shaped fuselage has a flat bottom and upswept rear section, with a stepped cockpit. The fuselage comprises two areas: the cockpit and the cargo compartment. The cargo compartment can carry 18 passengers and their luggage, or 16 parachutists fully equiped, or 2000kg (4400lb) of cargo, including road vehicles. For medical evacuations, 12 stretches and two seats can be mounted. Its cabin, open along the whole of the length of the plane, is complemented by the rear ramp which enables different logistic transport tasks to be carried out. The rear ramp can be opened while on the ground to load and unload; or in flight, for the launching of cargo, survival equipment or paratroopers.

SPECIFICATIONS

Primary Role:	STOL, light utility transport
Crew:	2
Contractor:	CASA
Length:	15.18m (49.75ft)
Wingspan:	19.12m (62.3ft)
Height:	6.29m (20.63ft)
Maximum Take-off Weight:	8100kg (17,820lb)
Powerplant:	2 x TPE331-10R-513C turboprops
Thrust:	1342kg (2952lb) each
Maximum Speed:	370km/h (231mph)
Ceiling:	9900m (32,480ft)
Range:	2680km (1675 miles)
Armament:	none
Systems:	electronic flight instruments system (EFIS), ESM, ECM, ELINT, COMINT
Date Deployed:	1972

JA 37 VIGGEN

In December 1961, the Swedish government approved the development of Aircraft System 37, the Viggen. The basic platform was the AJ 37 attack aircraft, to be followed by the S 37 reconnaissance version and JA 37 fighter. The new aircraft had a novel and advanced aerodynamic configuration to meet the short take-off and landing (STOL) and other performance requirements demanded of Swedish military aircraft: a fixed foreplane with flaps was mounted ahead of and slightly above the delta main wing. On 8 February 1967 the first prototype of the Saab 37 Viggen family made its maiden flight. In April 1968, the government authorized Viggen production and the first aircraft was delivered to the air force in July 1971. A total of 329 aircraft were eventually built in attack, trainer, two reconnaissance versions and the more powerful fighter variant that included new avionics, new air-to-air missiles (AAMs) and Europe's first pulse doppler radar. The last of 329 Viggens, a JA 37 fighter version, was delivered from Saab in Linköping to the Swedish Air Force in 1990. Since then, the Viggen has undergone several upgrades, the latest being Model D for the fighter version, which includes communication and weapon systems similar to those found in the Gripen. The Viggen has served the air force well for over 30 years.

SPECIFICATIONS

Primary Role:	*multirole fighter*
Crew:	*1*
Contractor:	*Saab*
Length:	*15.58m (51.1ft)*
Wingspan:	*10.6m (34.75ft)*
Height:	*5.9m (19.3ft)*
Maximum Take-off Weight:	*17,000kg (37,478lb)*
Powerplant:	*1 x Flygmotor RM8B turbofan*
Thrust:	*12,776kg (28,108lb)*
Maximum Speed:	*2250km/h (1406mph)*
Ceiling:	*18,300m (60,00ft)*
Range:	*2000km (1250 miles)*
Armament:	*1 x 30mm cannon, RB71, RB74 AAMs; bombs; RBS 15F anti-ship missile,*
Systems:	*ECM, countermeasures pod, ECCM*
Date Deployed:	*1971*

JAS39 GRIPEN

The Gripen fighter combines new avionics systems, modern materials, advanced aerodynamic design, a well-proven engine and fully integrated system to produce a highly capable, true multirole combat aircraft. The Gripen is the first Swedish aircraft that can be used for interception, ground-attack and reconnaissance (hence the Swedish abbreviation JAS – Fighter (J), Attack (A) and Reconnaissance (S) in Swedish) and is now successively replacing the Draken and Viggen. Gripen offers high agility, advanced target acquisition systems, low environmental signatures and a comprehensive electronic warfare (EW) suite. Currently, the Gripens used by the Swedish Air Force are armed with AIM-120 AMRAAM, AIM-9 Sidewinder, the Saab Dynamics RBS 15F for ship targets, and the Maverick ground-attack missile. A total of 204 aircraft in three batches have been ordered for the Swedish Air Force; the first batch of 30 aircraft has been completed. Deliveries from the second batch are ongoing, and comprise 96 one-seater and 14 two-seater aircraft. About 60 Gripens are in service with the Swedish Air Force. In June 1997, a third batch of 64 Gripens was approved by the Swedish government. This will take the total for the Swedish Air Force to 204. Production of batch three is scheduled for between 2002 and 2007.

SPECIFICATIONS

Primary Role:	multirole combat aircraft
Crew:	1
Contractor:	SAAB, Ericsson, Volvo, FFV Aerotech
Length:	14.1m (46.25ft)
Wingspan:	8.4m (27.5ft)
Height:	4.5 m (14.75ft)
Maximum Take-off Weight:	12,500kg (27,500lb)
Powerplant:	1 x Volvo Aero RM 12
Thrust:	8182kg (18,000lb)
Maximum Speed:	2450km/h (1531mph)
Ceiling:	14,021m (46,000ft)
Range:	unknown
Armament:	1 x 27mm gun, AMRAAM, Sidewinder, SRAAM AAMs, RBS 15F ASM
Systems:	pulse doppler radar, FLIR, infrared search and track
Date Deployed:	1997

S100B ARGUS

The Saab 340 is a Swedish twin-engined turboprop aircraft. An airborne early warning (AEW) version with a phased-array radar in a rectangular pod on top of the fuselage was developed in the early 1990s. In 1994 the first Saab 340 AEW & C was produced, and a year later it was re-designated S100B (S – *Spaning* – Reconnaissance) and given the official name Argus. The Swedish Air Force ordered six aircraft, four of which will be fitted with radar. Some are used by Japan as search and rescue aircraft. The Ericsson PS-890 Erieye radar uses an active array with 200 solid-state modules. Utilizing adaptive side lobe suppression, the look angle on each side is about 160 degrees. From its standard operational altitude of 6000m (19,685ft) the radar has a maximum range of 450km (279 miles). Against a fighter-sized target effective range is approximately 330km (205 miles). Seaborne targets can be detected at 320km (200 miles), though this is a function dependent on the aircraft's cruising height. The electronically scanned antenna can scan sectors of interest frequently while others are monitored, and a single sector can be scanned in different modes at the same time. The aircraft does not carry controllers (although it is large enough to do so), but functions as an airborne radar integrated with the total air defence network.

SPECIFICATIONS

Primary Role:	airborne early warning
Crew:	2–5
Contractor:	Saab-Scania Aktiebolag, Aerospace Division
Length:	19.7m (64.6ft)
Wingspan:	21.4m (70.3ft)
Height:	6.9m (22.8ft)
Maximum Take-off Weight:	13,181kg (29,000lb)
Powerplant:	2 x General Electric CT7-9B turboprops
Thrust:	2600kg (5720lb) each
Maximum Speed:	463km/h (288mph)
Ceiling:	7620m (4762 miles)
Range:	1300km (812 miles)
Armament:	none
Systems:	Ericsson PS-890 Erieye radar
Date Deployed:	1994

IDF

Taiwan produced the *Ching-kuo* Indigenous Defence Fighter (IDF) with extensive assistance from American corporations, led by General Dynamics. With a combat radius of 960km (600 miles) while carrying out armed reconnaissance and patrol missions, the IDF is capable of conducting pre-emptive raids and strikes at airports along the Chinese coast. Its main role is one of air superiority, but it is also capable of carrying "Hsiung Feng-II" missiles to attack targets at sea. Most of the IDFs are expected to be armed with the indigenously produced BVR Tien Chien-II (Sky Sword-II) air-to-air missile (AAM). The IDF has faced numerous developmental and operational problems since its inception in the 1980s. Nevertheless, its technical sophistication, with its fly-by-wire controls and blended wing-body design, is believed to be superior to any aircraft produced and deployed by China to date. By 1997 some 60 had been built, and production of all 130 IDFs has now been completed. The twin-engine IDF is similar to the F-16 except that it is slightly smaller and has a slightly shorter range. The IDF is a hybrid as far as its external appearance is concerned. The nose of the fighter is a replica of the US F-20A Tigershark, while its body, wings and vertical tail surface are apparently lifted from the F-16.

SPECIFICATIONS

Primary Role:	*air superiority fighter*
Crew:	*1*
Contractor:	*AIDC*
Length:	*13.26m (43.5ft)*
Wingspan:	*9m (29.5ft)*
Height:	*4.04m (13.25ft)*
Maximum Take-off Weight:	*12,273kg (27,000lb)*
Powerplant:	*2 x ITEC (Garrett/AIDC) TFE1042-70 turbofans*
Thrust:	*4300kg (9460lb) each*
Maximum Speed:	*1275km/h (797mph)*
Ceiling:	*16,760m (54,987ft)*
Range:	*unknown*
Armament:	*1 x 20mm cannon;S ky Sword I and II AAMs; Hsiung Feng II ASM*
Systems:	*GD-53 pulse doppler radar, IRWR*
Date Deployed:	*1994*

A-4 SKYHAWK

The US Marine Corps' A-4 Skyhawk is a lightweight, single-engine attack aircraft. The mission of an A-4 squadron is to attack and destroy surface targets in support of the landing force commander, escort helicopters, and conduct other operations as directed. Developed in the early 1950s, the A-4 Skyhawk was originally designated the A-4D. It was a lightweight, daylight only, nuclear capable strike aircraft for use in large numbers from aircraft carriers. There are numerous models of the A-4 in use. The A-4M and the TA-4F (trainer) are currently used by Marine Corps Reserve squadrons. All models have two internally mounted 20mm cannons, and are capable of delivering conventional and nuclear weapons under day and night visual meteorological conditions. The A-4M uses a head-up display (HUD) and computer-aided delivery of its bomb load with the angle rate bombing system. The Marine Reserve has two squadrons of A-4s with 12 aircraft each. Additionally, each squadron has two TA-4 aircraft. The A-4 aircraft is one of the most effective and versatile light attack aircraft produced. Though the Skyhawk is over 30 years old, export models are still highly regarded and undergoing modern avionics, weapons and engine upgrades to maintain their flying prowess into the twenty-first century.

SPECIFICATIONS

Primary Role:	*attack aircraft*
Crew:	*1*
Contractor:	*McDonnell Douglas*
Length:	*12.98m (42.58ft)*
Wingspan:	*8.38m (27.5ft)*
Height:	*4.66m (15.25ft)*
Maximum Take-off Weight:	*11,113kg (24,500lb)*
Powerplant:	*1 x J-52-P-408A turbojet*
Thrust:	*5091kg (11,200lb)*
Maximum Speed:	*1052km/h (657mph)*
Ceiling:	*12,880m (42,257ft)*
Range:	*3225km (2016 miles)*
Armament:	*2 x 20mm cannon; Sidewinder, Shrike and Walleye missiles; AGM-65 Maverick ASM*
Systems:	*TACAN, IFF, HUD, AN/AVQ-24, AN/ASN-41*
Date Deployed:	*1962*

A-10 THUNDERBOLT

The A-10 and OA-10 Thunderbolt IIs were the first air force aircraft specially designed for close air support of ground forces. They are simple, effective and survivable twin-engine jet aircraft that can be used against all ground targets, their seven-barrelled Gatling gun being particularly potent. The primary mission of the A-10 is to provide day and night close air combat support for friendly land forces; its secondary mission is supporting search and rescue and Special Forces operations. Specific survivability features include a titanium armour-plated cockpit, redundant flight control system separated by fuel tanks, manual reversion mode for flight controls, foam-filled fuel tanks, ballistic foam void fillers, and a redundant primary structure providing "get home" capability after being hit. Design simplicity, ease of access and left-to-right interchangeable components make the A/OA-10 easily maintainable and suitable for deployment at advanced bases. It has excellent manoeuvrability at low air speeds and altitudes, and is a highly accurate weapons-delivery platform. Its wide combat radius and short take-off and landing (STOL) capability permit operations in and out of locations near frontlines. Using night vision goggles, Thunderbolt pilots can conduct their missions during darkness with ease.

SPECIFICATIONS

Primary Role:	close air support
Crew:	1
Contractor:	Fairchild Republic
Length:	16.16m (53ft)
Wingspan:	17.42m (57.15ft)
Height:	4.42m (14.5ft)
Maximum Take-off Weight:	22,950kg (51,000lb)
Powerplant:	2 x GE TF34-GE-100 turbofans
Thrust:	4120kg (9065lb) each
Maximum Speed:	672km/h (420mph)
Ceiling:	13,636m (45,000ft)
Range:	1280km (800 miles)
Armament:	1 x 30mm gun; Mk 82, Mk 84, CBU-52, CBU-58, CBU-71, CBU-87, CBU-89 bombs, AGM-65 Maverick ASM
Systems:	LASTE, GCAS
Date Deployed:	1976

AC-130H SPECTRE

The AC-130H Spectre gunship's primary missions are close air support, air interdiction and armed reconnaissance. These heavily armed aircraft incorporate side-firing weapons integrated with sophisticated sensor, navigation and fire-control systems to provide surgical firepower or area saturation during extended periods, at night and in adverse weather. The AC-130H is an excellent fire support platform with outstanding capabilities. With its extremely accurate fire-control system, it can place 105mm, 40mm and 25mm munitions on target with first-round accuracy. The new AC-130U Spectre gunship is being fielded as a replacement for the AC-130A aircraft. The AC-130U airframe is integrated with an armour protection system (APS), high-resolution sensors, infrared detection set (IDS), avionics and EW systems, and an armament suite consisting of side-firing, trainable 25mm, 40mm and 105mm guns. The AC-130U is the most complex aircraft weapon system in the world today: it has more than 609,000 lines of software code in its mission computers and avionics systems. The newest addition to the command fleet, it can provide surgical firepower or area saturation during extended loiter periods, against targets that include troops, fortifications and armoured vehicles.

SPECIFICATIONS

Primary Role:	*close air support*
Crew:	*14*
Contractor:	*Lockheed Aircraft Corporation*
Length:	*29.8m (97.75ft)*
Wingspan:	*40.4m (132.5ft)*
Height:	*11.7m (38.5ft)*
Maximum Take-off Weight:	*70,454kg (155,000lb)*
Powerplant:	*4 x T56-A-15 turboprops*
Thrust:	*6724kg (14,793lb) each*
Maximum Speed:	*480km/h (300mph)*
Ceiling:	*7576m (25,000ft)*
Range:	*2400km (1500 miles)*
Armament:	*2 x 20mm cannons, 1 x 40mm, 1 x 105mm*
Systems:	*DIRCM, AN/AAR-44 infrared warning receiver, AN/AAR-47 missile warning system*
Date Deployed:	*1972*

AV-8B HARRIER

The AV-8B V/STOL strike aircraft was designed to replace the AV-8A and the A-4M light attack aircraft. The Marine Corps had a requirement for a V/STOL light attack force since the late 1950s. Combining tactical mobility, responsiveness, reduced operating costs and flexibility, both afloat and ashore, V/STOL aircraft are particularly well-suited to the special combat and expeditionary requirements of the Marines. The AV-8BII+ features the APG-65 radar common to the F/A-18, as well as all previous systems and features common to the AV-8BII. The mission of the V/STOL squadron is to attack and destroy surface and air targets, to escort helicopters, and to conduct other such air operations as may be directed. It is operational with the US Marine Corps, the Spanish Navy and the Italian Navy. Weapons include the air-to-air AMRAAM and Sparrow missiles, air-to-surface AGM-65 Maverick missiles, and anti-ship Harpoon and Sea Eagle missiles, 25mm cannon and a range of bombs and rockets. The AGM-65 Maverick missile is installed on the Italian Harrier II Plus. The Harrier II Plus is also capable of deploying the Sea Eagle anti-ship missile, which is a fire-and-forget sea-skimming missile also carried on the Sea Harrier, and the air-launch version of the AGM-84 Harpoon surface strike missile.

SPECIFICATIONS

Primary Role:	*close air support, interceptor*
Crew:	*1*
Contractor:	*McDonnell Douglas*
Length:	*14.12m (46.3ft)*
Wingspan:	*9.25m (30.3ft)*
Height:	*3.55m (11.6ft)*
Maximum Take-off Weight:	*14,061kg (31,000lb)*
Powerplant:	*1 x Pegasus F402-RR-406 turbofan*
Thrust:	*10,091kg (22,200lb)*
Maximum Speed:	*1065km/h (666mph)*
Ceiling:	*15,000m (49,212ft)*
Range:	*2408km (1505 miles)*
Armament:	*1 x 25mm gun system, AGM-65, AIM-9L/M Sidewinder, GBU-12, GBU-16, CBU-99/100*
Systems:	*NAVFLIR, ARBS, AN/APG-65 radar system*
Date Deployed:	*1993*

B-1B LANCER

The B-1B is a multirole, long-range bomber capable of penetrating present and predicted sophisticated enemy defences. It can perform a variety of missions, including that of a conventional weapons carrier for theatre operations. The swing-wing design and turbofan engines not only provide greater range and high speed at low levels, they also enhance the bomber's overall survivability. Wing sweep at the full-forward position allows a short take-off and a fast base-escape profile for airfields under attack. Once airborne, the wings are positioned for maximum cruise distance or high-speed penetration. Differences between the B-1B and its predecessor, the B-1A of the 1970s, include a simplified engine inlet, modified over-wing fairing and relocated pilot tubes. The B-1B was structurally redesigned to increase its gross take-off weight from 179,545kg to 216,818kg (395,000lb to 477,000lb). This added take-off weight capacity, in addition to a moveable bulkhead between the forward and intermediate weapons bay, allows the B-1B Lancer to carry a wide variety of nuclear and conventional munitions. The most significant changes, however, are in the avionics, with an overall low-radar cross-section, automatic terrain-following high-speed penetration, and extremely precise weapons delivery.

SPECIFICATIONS

Primary Role:	*long-range bomber*
Crew:	*4*
Contractor:	*Rockwell, North American Aircraft*
Length:	*44.5m (146ft)*
Wingspan:	*41.8m (137ft) to 24.1m (79ft)*
Height:	*10.4m (34ft)*
Maximum Take-off Weight:	*216,818kg (477,000lb)*
Powerplant:	*4 x F-101-GE-102 turbofans*
Thrust:	*13,500kg (29,700lb) each*
Maximum Speed:	*1440km/h (900mph)*
Ceiling:	*9000m (30,000ft)*
Range:	*12,000km (7500 miles)*
Armament:	*8 x cruise missiles, freefall nuclear & conventional bombs*
Systems:	*JDAM, AN/ALQ 161A defensive avionics*
Date Deployed:	*1986*

B-2 SPIRIT

The B-2 programme was initiated in 1981, principally for strategic bombing missions against targets in Eastern Europe and Soviet Russia. With the fall of the Soviet Union, the emphasis of B-2 development was changed to conventional operations and the production number was reduced to 20 aircraft. The B-2's "stealth" characteristics give it the unique ability to penetrate an enemy's most sophisticated defences and threaten its most valued, heavily defended targets. The blending of low-observable technologies with high aerodynamic efficiency and large payload gives the B-2 important advantages over existing bombers. Its low observability gives it greater freedom of action at high altitudes, thus increasing its range and giving better field of view for the aircraft's sensors. Its low observability is derived from a combination of reduced infrared, acoustic, electromagnetic, visual and radar signatures. These signatures make it difficult for defensive systems to detect, track and engage the B-2. Many aspects of the low-observability manufacturing process remain classified; however, the Spirit's composite materials, special coatings and flying wing design all contribute to its "stealthiness". B-2s, in a conventional role, staging from Whiteman Air Force Base, Diego Garcia and Guam can cover the entire world with just one refuelling.

SPECIFICATIONS

Primary Role:	*multirole heavy bomber*
Crew:	*2*
Contractor:	*Northrop Grumman*
Length:	*20.9m (69ft)*
Wingspan:	*52.12m (172ft)*
Height:	*5.1m (17ft)*
Maximum Take-off Weight:	*152,954kg (336,500lb)*
Powerplant:	*4 x F-118-GE-100 turbofans*
Thrust:	*7864kg (17,300lb) each*
Maximum Speed:	*classified*
Ceiling:	*15,240m (50,000ft)*
Range:	*12,223km (7639 miles)*
Armament:	*combination of 16 B61, B83, AGM–129 ACM, CBU-87, GBU-27, JDAM, TSSAM*
Systems:	*Line-of-Sight (LOS) data*
Date Deployed:	*1993*

B-52 STRATOFORTRESS

The B-52H is the primary nuclear bomber in the USAF inventory. Only the H model is still in the air force inventory and all are assigned to the Air Combat Command. Starting in 1989, an on-going modification has incorporated the global positioning system, heavy stores adaptor beams for carrying 909kg (2000lb) munitions and additional smart weapons capability. In a conventional conflict, the B-52H can perform air interdiction, offensive counter-air and maritime operations. During Desert Storm, for example, B-52s delivered 40 percent of all the weapons dropped by Allied forces. It is highly effective when used for ocean surveillance, and can assist the US Navy in anti-ship and mine-laying operations. All aircraft are being modified to carry the AGM-142 Raptor missile and AGM-84 Harpoon anti-ship missile. There is a proposal under consideration to re-engine the remaining B-52H aircraft to extend their service life. If implemented, the B-52 will serve until 2025. However, the limiting factor of the B-52's service life is the economic limit of the aircraft's upper wing surface, calculated to have a life of 32,500 to 37,500 flight hours. Based on the projected economic service life and forecast mishap rates, the air force will be unable to maintain the requirement of 62 B-52 aircraft by 2044, after 84 years in service.

SPECIFICATIONS

Primary Role:	*heavy bomber*
Crew:	*5*
Contractor:	*Boeing*
Length:	*48.5m (159.1ft)*
Wingspan:	*56.4m (185ft)*
Height:	*12.4m (40.6ft)*
Maximum Take-off Weight:	*221,818kg (488,000lb)*
Powerplant:	*8 x TF33-P-3/103 turbofans*
Thrust:	*7650kg (17,000lb) each*
Maximum Speed:	*1040km/h (650mph)*
Ceiling:	*15,240m (50,000ft)*
Range:	*14,080km (8800 miles)*
Armament:	*27 internal weapons, 18 external weapons*
Systems:	*AN/ANS-136, AN/APN-224, AN/ASN-134, AN/APQ-156, AN/ASQ-175 AN/AYQ-10*
Date Deployed:	*1955*

C-2A GREYHOUND

The C-2A Greyhound twin-engine cargo aircraft was designed to land on aircraft carriers. In 1984 a contract was awarded for 39 new C-2A aircraft. Dubbed the Reprocured C-2A due to its similarity to the original, the new aircraft include substantial improvements in airframe and avionics systems. All the older C-2As were phased out in 1987, and the last of the new models was delivered in 1990. The avionics block upgrades for the C-2A(R) provide increased reliability and maintainability. A limited development test was conducted on the C-2A(R), due to the minor differences to the previous C-2A. Development test and evaluation and operational test and evaluation were performed by the Naval Air Warfare Center Aircraft Division from June 1985 to February 1986. These aircraft have a 4545kg (10,000lb) payload capacity and operate from forward area air stations in support of Atlantic and Pacific fleet operations. The aircraft's large aft door ramp and powered winch promote a fast turn-around time via straight-in rear loading and unloading. Special missions have been developed which employ the C-2A. These missions include personnel, combat rubber raiding craft (CRRC) and air cargo drops. The CRRC drops entail disembarking a team of divers and their equipment while airborne.

SPECIFICATIONS

Primary Role:	carrier cargo aircraft
Crew:	4
Contractor:	Grumann Aerospace
Length:	17.3m (57.75ft)
Wingspan:	24.69m (81ftt)
Height:	5m (17ft)
Maximum Take-off Weight:	25,909kg (57,000lb)
Powerplant:	2 x T-56-A-425 turboprops
Thrust:	7000kg (15,400lb) each
Maximum Speed:	563km/h (352mph)
Ceiling:	9100m (30,000ft)
Range:	2392km (1495 miles)
Armament:	none
Systems:	pulse doppler radar, two carrier approach systems
Date Deployed:	1965

C-5A/B GALAXY

The C-5 Galaxy is a heavy cargo transport designed to provide strategic airlift for the deployment and supply of combat and support forces. The C-5 can carry unusually large and heavy cargo over intercontinental ranges at jet speeds. Features unique to the C-5 include the forward cargo door and ramp and the aft cargo door system and ramp. These features allow drive-on/drive-off loading and unloading, as well as loading and unloading from either end of the cargo compartment. The C-5's kneeling capability also facilitates and expedites these operations by lowering cargo ramps for truck loading and reduces ramp angles for loading and unloading vehicles. The C-5's floor does not have tread-ways and the "floor-bearing pressure" is the same over the entire floor. The C-5A/B can carry up to 36 pallets. The troop compartment is located in the aircraft's upper deck. It is self-contained with a galley, two lavatories and 73 available passenger seats. Another 267 airline seats can be installed on the cargo compartment floor to give a maximum carrying capacity of 329 troops including air crew. At present, the C-5 has the highest operating cost of any military aircraft. For example, the A model requires 46 maintenance man hours per flying hour, with 16.7 maintenance man hours per flying hour for the B model.

SPECIFICATIONS

Primary Role:	strategic airlift
Crew:	6
Contractor:	Lockheed-Georgia
Length:	75.3m (247ft)
Wingspan:	67.9m (222.75ft)
Height:	19.8m (65ft)
Maximum Take-off Weight:	381,818kg (840,000lb)
Powerplant:	4 x General Electric TF39-GE-1C turbofans
Thrust:	18,450kg (41,000lb) each
Maximum Speed:	866km/h (541mph)
Ceiling:	10,303m (34,000ft)
Range:	9504km (5940 miles)
Armament:	none
Systems:	Malfunction Detection Analysis and Recording System
Date Deployed:	1970

C-17 GLOBEMASTER III

The C-17 Globemaster is capable of deploying troops and all types of cargo to main operating bases or directly to forward bases in the deployment area. The design of this cargo aircraft lets it operate on small, austere airfields. For example, the C-17 can take off and land on runways as short as 914m (3000ft) and as narrow as 27.4m (90ft) wide. Even on such narrow runways, the C-17 can turn around by using its backing capability while performing a three-point star turn. The manufacturers have made maximum use of off-the-shelf and commercial equipment, including air force standardized avionics. The design of the cargo compartment allows the C-17 to carry a wide range of vehicles, palleted cargo, paratroopers, airdrop loads and aeromedical evacuees. The cargo compartment has a sufficiently large cross-section to transport large wheeled and tracked vehicles, tanks, helicopters such as the AH-64 Apache, artillery and weapons such as the Patriot missile system. The C-17 is capable of carrying out an airdrop of outsized firepower such as the Sheridan light tank or Bradley fighting vehicle if the Bradley is refitted to be airdrop capable. Three Bradley armoured vehicles comprise one deployment load on the C-17. The US Army M-1 main battle tank can also be carried with other vehicles.

SPECIFICATIONS

Primary Role:	cargo and troop transport
Crew:	3
Contractor:	Boeing (McDonnell Douglas Corporation)
Length:	53.04m (173.9ft)
Wingspan:	51.81m (170.75ft)
Height:	16.79m (55ft)
Maximum Take-off Weight:	265,909kg (585,000lb)
Powerplant:	4 x Pratt & Whitney F117-PW-100 turbofans
Thrust:	18,590kg (40,900lb) each
Maximum Speed:	800km/h (500mph)
Ceiling:	13,716m (45,000ft)
Range:	unlimited with in-flight refuelling
Armament:	none
Systems:	AN/AAR-47 missile warning system
Date Deployed:	1993

C-20

The various versions of the C-20 are military modifications of the commercial Gulfstream aircraft. The C-20 aircraft provide distinguished visitor (DV) airlift for military and government officials, offering worldwide access while including a communications suite which supports worldwide secure voice and data communications for the DV and his staff. In June 1983 it was chosen as the replacement aircraft for the C-140B Jetstar, and three A models were delivered to the 89th Airlift Wing at Andrews Air Force Base under a cost-saving accelerated purchase plan. The three C-20As at Andrews were subsequently transferred to Ramstein Air Base, Germany. Seven B-model C-20s fly special air missions from Andrews. The primary difference between the C-20A and B models is the electrical system and avionics package. C-20B aircraft will reach their 20,000-hour service life in about 2014. The C-20D is a Gulfstream III aircraft capable of all-weather, long-range, high speed non-stop flights between airports. The C-20D aircraft are operated by Fleet Logistics Support Wing Detachment. The C-20G is a Gulfstream IV aircraft capable of all-weather, long-range, high speed flights between airports. They are operated by the Fleet Logistics Support Squadron Four Eight (VR-48) and the Marine Air Support Detachment (MASD).

SPECIFICATIONS

Primary Role:	operational support airlift, special air missions
Crew:	5
Contractor:	Gulfstream Aerospace
Length:	25.35m (83.16ft)
Wingspan:	23.71m (77.78in)
Height:	7.46m (24.5ft)
Maximum Take-off Weight:	31,682kg (69,700lb)
Powerplant:	2 x Rolls-Royce Spey MK511-8 turbofans
Thrust:	5182kg (11,400lb) each
Maximum Speed:	922km/h (576mph)
Ceiling:	13,715m (44,997ft)
Range:	7544km (4715 miles)
Armament:	none
Systems:	Honeywell Primus Avionics Suite
Date Deployed:	1983

C-130 HERCULES

The C-130 Hercules is capable of operating from rough airstrips and is the prime transport for paradropping troops and equipment into hostile areas. Basic and specialized versions perform a diversity of roles, including airlift support, DEW (Distant Early Warning) Line and Arctic ice re-supply, aeromedical missions, aerial spray missions, fire-fighting duties for the US Forest Service, and natural disaster relief missions. There are several variants: the initial production model was the C-130A; the C-130B introduced Allison T56-A-7 turboprops; and several A models, redesignated C-130D, were modified with wheel-ski landing gear for service in the Arctic. The C-130E is an extended-range development of the B, with two underwing fuel tanks and increased range and endurance capabilities. Similar to the E model, the C-130H has updated T56-A-T5 turboprops, a redesigned outer wing, updated avionics and other minor improvements. The the C-130J climbs faster and higher, flies farther at a higher cruise speed, and takes off and lands in a shorter distance. The C-130 can accommodate 92 combat troops or 64 fully equipped paratroopers on side-facing seats. For medical evacuations, it carries 74 litter patients and two medical attendants. Paratroopers exit the aircraft through two doors on either side of the aircraft or via the rear ramp.

SPECIFICATIONS

Primary Role:	transport
Crew:	5
Contractor:	Lockheed Martin
Length:	29.3m (97.75ft)
Wingspan:	39.7m (132.5ft)
Height:	11.4m (38.25ft)
Maximum Take-off Weight:	69,750kg (155,000lb)
Powerplant:	4 x T56-A-15 turboprops
Thrust:	6724kg (14,793lb) each
Maximum Speed:	598km/h (374mph)
Ceiling:	10,000m (33,000ft)
Range:	3770km (2356 miles)
Armament:	none
Systems:	GPS/INS, E-TCAS, SKE2000 station keeping system and an Instrument Landing System (ILS)
Date Deployed:	1955

C-141B STARLIFTER

The Starlifter can airlift combat forces, equipment and supplies, and deliver them on the ground or by airdrop, using paratrooper doors on each side and a rear loading ramp. It can be used for low-altitude delivery of paratroopers and equipment, and high-altitude delivery of paratroopers. It can also airdrop equipment and supplies using the container delivery system. It is the first aircraft designed to be compatible with the 463L Material Handling System, which permits the off-loading of 30,600kg (68,000lb) of cargo, refuelling and reloading a full load, all in less than an hour. The C-141 has an all-weather landing system, pressurized cabin and crew station. Its cargo compartment can easily be modified to perform around 30 different missions. About 200 troops or 155 fully equipped paratroopers can sit in canvas side-facing seats, or 166 troops in rear-facing airline seats. Rollers in the aircraft floor allow quick and easy cargo pallet loading. When palletized cargo is not being carried, the rollers can be turned over to leave a smooth, flat surface for the loading of vehicles. Several C-141s have been modified to carry the Minuteman missile in its special container, up to a total weight of 41,400kg (92,000lb). Some C-141s have intra-formation positioning for maintaining formation regardless of visibility.

SPECIFICATIONS

Primary Role:	*long-range transport*
Crew:	*6*
Contractor:	*Lockheed-Georgia*
Length:	*51m (168.3ft)*
Wingspan:	*48.5m (160ft)*
Height:	*11.9m (39.25ft)*
Maximum Take-off Weight:	*146,864kg (323,100lb)*
Powerplant:	*4 x Pratt & Whitney TF33-P-7 turbofans*
Thrust:	*9205kg (20,250lb) each*
Maximum Speed:	*800km/h (500mph)*
Ceiling:	*12,424m (41,000ft)*
Range:	*4000km (2500 miles)*
Armament:	*none*
Systems:	*Container Delivery System (CDS), 463L Material Handling System*
Date Deployed:	*1964*

E-2C HAWKEYE

The E-2C Hawkeye is the US Navy's all-weather, carrier-based tactical airborne warning and control system platform for the carrier battle group. Additional missions include surface surveillance coordination, strike and interceptor control, search and rescue guidance and communications relay. An integral component of the carrier air wing, the E-2C carries three primary sensors: radar, IFF and a passive detection system. These sensors are integrated through a general-purpose computer that enables the E-2C to provide early warning, threat analysis and control of counter action against air and surface targets. The E-2C incorporates the latest solid-state electronics. There is currently one squadron of four Hawkeyes in each carrier air wing. The large 7.3m- (24ft-) diameter circular antenna radome above the rear fuselage gives the E-2C its distinctive profile. The radome houses the AN/APA-171 antenna, which rotates at 5–6 revolutions per minute. The AN/APS-145 radar is capable of tracking more than 2000 targets and controlling the interception of 40 hostile targets. The radar's total radiation aperture-control antenna reduces sidelobes and is robust against electronic countermeasures (ECM). It is capable of detecting aircraft at ranges greater than 550 km (344 miles).

SPECIFICATIONS

Primary Role:	carrier AEW aircraft
Crew:	5
Contractor:	Grumman
Length:	17.5m (57.41ft)
Wingspan:	24.6m (80.7ft)
Height:	5.6m (18.37ft)
Maximum Take-off Weight:	24,161kg (53,154lb)
Powerplant:	2 x T56-A-427 turboprops
Thrust:	7606kg (16,733lb) each
Maximum Speed:	626km/h (389mph)
Ceiling:	11,300m (37,073ft)
Range:	3000km (1875 miles)
Armament:	none
Systems:	AN/ASN-92 CAINS, AN/APS-145 radar, AN/UYQ-70 advanced display system
Date Deployed:	1973

E-3 SENTRY

The E-3 Airborne Warning and Control System (AWACS) aircraft carries out airborne surveillance, and command, control and communications (C3) functions for both tactical and air defence forces. The E3 look-down radar has a 360-degree view of the horizon, and at operating altitudes has a range of more than 320km (200 miles). The radar can detect and track air and sea targets simultaneously. In a tactical role, the E-3 can detect and track hostile aircraft operating at low altitudes over any terrain, and can identify and control friendly aircraft in the same airspace. In the strategic defence role, the E-3 provides the means to detect, identify, track and intercept airborne threats. The basic E-3 is a militarized version of the Boeing 707-320B commercial jet airframe, distinguished by the addition of a large, rotating radome containing the main radar, identification friend or foe (IFF) and Tactical Data Information Link-Control (TADIL-C) antennas. The layout of the equipment in the fuselage is arranged in bays with areas allocated for communications, signal and data processing, command and control, navigation and target identification systems. The signal and data processing is carried out on a high-speed IBM 4PiCC-1 computer. The aircraft is equipped with 14 command and control consoles.

SPECIFICATIONS

Primary Role:	AWACS
Crew:	17
Contractor:	Boeing
Length:	46.62m (152.9ft)
Wingspan:	44.43m (145.75ft)
Height:	12.5m (41.75ft)
Maximum Take-off Weight:	151,955kg (335,000lb)
Powerplant:	4 x TF-33-PW-1 00 A turbofans
Thrust:	9545kg (21,000lb) each
Maximum Speed:	800km/h (500mph)
Ceiling:	10,670m (35,000ft)
Range:	9250km (5781 miles)
Armament:	none
Systems:	AN/APY-1/2 radar, Data Processing Functional Group, Tactical Data Information Link
Date Deployed:	1977

E-4B NAOC

The E-4B serves as the National Airborne Operations Center (NAOC) for the National Command Authorities. In cases of national emergency or destruction of ground command control centres, the aircraft provides a highly surviveable, command, control and communications centre to direct US forces, execute emergency war orders and coordinate actions by civil authorities. There are only four E-4B aircraft, with one constantly on alert. The E-4B, a militarized version of the Boeing 747-200, is a four-engine long-range, high-altitude aircraft capable of being refuelled in flight. The main deck is divided into six functional areas: a National Command Authorities' work area, conference room, briefing room, an operations team work area, communications area and rest areas. The E-4B has electromagnetic pulse protection, an electrical system designed to support advanced electronics and a wide variety of new communications equipment. Other improvements include nuclear and thermal effects shielding, acoustic control, an improved technical control facility and an upgraded air-conditioning system for cooling electrical components. An advanced satellite communications system also improves worldwide communications among strategic and tactical satellite systems and the airborne operations centre.

SPECIFICATIONS

Primary Role:	airborne operations centre
Crew:	up to 114
Contractor:	Boeing
Length:	70.5m (231.3ft)
Wingspan:	59.7m (195.6ft)
Height:	19.3m (63.5ft)
Maximum Take-off Weight:	360,000kg (800,000lb)
Powerplant:	4 x CF6-50E2 turbofans
Thrust:	23,863kg (52,500lb) each
Maximum Speed:	969km/h (602mph)
Ceiling:	9091m (30,000ft)
Range:	unknown
Armament:	none
Systems:	electromagnetic pulse protection, nuclear and thermal effects shielding, acoustic control
Date Deployed:	1980

E-6 MERCURY

The E-6 is the airborne portion of the TACAMO (take charge and move out) Communications System. It provides surviveable communication links between the National Command Authority (NCA) and strategic forces. The E-6 is a version of the commercial Boeing 707 aircraft: a long-range, air-refuelable aircraft equipped with four CFM-56-2A-2 high bypass ratio fan/jet engines with thrust reversers. The aircraft is electromagnetic pulse hardened. It has an endurance of over 15 hours without refuelling and a maximum endurance of 72 hours with inflight refuelling. The E-6B is a dual-mission aircraft capable of fulfiling either the E-6A mission or the airborne strategic command post mission and is equipped with an airborne launch control system (ALCS), which is capable of launching US land-based intercontinental ballistic missiles. The first E-6B aircraft was accepted in December 1997 and the E-6B assumed its dual operational mission in October 1998. The E-6 fleet will be completely modified to the E-6B configuration by 2003. In the TACAMO role, the E-6 flies independent random operations from various deployed sites for approximately 15-day intervals, and each deployed crew is self-supporting except for fuel and perishables. Mission commitment is in the Atlantic and Pacific regions.

SPECIFICATIONS

Primary Role:	*airborne command post*
Crew:	*14*
Contractor:	*Boeing*
Length:	*45.8m (150.3ft)*
Wingspan:	*45.2m (148.3ft)*
Height:	*12.9m (42.5ft)*
Maximum Take-off Weight:	*155,000kg (341,000lb)*
Powerplant:	*4 x CFM-56-2A-2 high bypass turbofans*
Thrust:	*10,900kg (23,980lb) each*
Maximum Speed:	*960km/h (600mph)*
Ceiling:	*12,192m (40,000ft)*
Range:	*12,144km (7590 miles)*
Armament:	*none*
Systems:	*TACAMO suite, WING-TIP pods, trailing wire antenna, and four 75-KNA generators*
Date Deployed:	*1989*

E-8C JOINT STARS

The Joint Surveillance Target Attack Radar System (Joint STARS) is a long-range, air-to-ground surveillance system designed to locate, classify and track ground targets in all weather conditions. It has a range of more than 250 km (150 miles). These capabilities make Joint STARS effective for dealing with any contingency, whether actual or impending military aggression, international treaty verification, or border violation. Joint STARS consists of an airborne platform – an E-8C aircraft with a multi-mode radar system – and US Army mobile Ground Station Modules (GSMs). The E-8C, a modified Boeing 707, carries a phased-array radar antenna in a radome under the forward part of the fuselage. The radar is capable of providing targeting and battle management data to all Joint STARS operators, both in the aircraft and in ground station modules. These operators, in turn, can call on aircraft, missiles or artillery for fire support. JSTARS aircraft have 17 operations consoles and one navigation/self-defence console. A console operator can carry out sector search focusing on smaller sectors and automatically track selected targets. Signal processing techniques are implemented through four high-speed data processors, each capable of performing more than 600 million operations per second.

SPECIFICATIONS

Primary Role:	ground surveillance
Crew:	up to 34
Contractor:	Northrop Grumman
Length:	46.6m (152.9ft)
Wingspan:	44.4 m (145.75ft)
Height:	12.9m (42.5ft)
Maximum Take-off Weight:	152,727kg (336,000lb)
Powerplant:	4 x JT3D-3B turbojets
Thrust:	8182kg (18,000lb) each
Maximum Speed:	945km/h (590mph)
Ceiling:	12,802m (42,000ft)
Range:	unknown
Armament:	none
Systems:	radar, UHF radios, HF radios, VHF radios, SINCGARS, SATCOM, SCDL, JTIDS
Date Deployed:	1996

E-767 AWACS

The Boeing E-767 AWACS (Airborne Warning and Control System) has been selected by the Japanese government to carry out airborne surveillance and command and control operations for tactical and air defence forces. The surveillance system is based on a flexible, multi-mode radar which enables AWACS to separate maritime and airborne targets from ground and sea clutter radar returns. Production of the Boeing 707 airframe ended in May 1991. Following studies of the most suitable follow-on aircraft for the AWACS mission, Boeing announced in December 1991 that it would offer a modified 767 as the platform for the system. The first two aircraft were delivered to the government of Japan in March 1998, and the final two aircraft were delivered in January 1999. All four aircraft entered service with the Japanese Air Self-Defence Force (JASDF) in May 2000. The main AWACS operations cabin behind the flight deck is laid out in equipment bays for communications, data and signal processing, navigation and identification equipment. The AWACS officers and operator stations are equipped with Hazeltine command and control consoles fitted with high-resolution colour displays. The main signal and data processing computer, the CC-2E, has a main storage capacity of over three million words.

SPECIFICATIONS

Primary Role:	AWACS
Crew:	21
Contractor:	Boeing
Length:	48.51m (159.2ft)
Wingspan:	47.57m (156.1ft)
Height:	15.85m (52ft)
Maximum Take-off Weight:	175,000kg (385,000lb)
Powerplant:	2 x General Electric CF6-80C2B6FA turbofans
Thrust:	27,955kg (61,500lb) each
Maximum Speed:	800km/h (500mph)
Ceiling:	12,222m (40,100ft)
Range:	10,370km (6481 miles)
Armament:	none
Systems:	AN/APY-2 radar, Lockheed Martin CC-2E signal and data processing computer
Date Deployed:	2000

EA-6B PROWLER

The EA-6B Prowler is the primary tactical jamming aircraft of the US Navy, US Air Force and the US Marine Corps. The aircraft operates from aircraft carriers and from forward land bases. Its mission is to accompany the strike forces and to carry out armed reconnaissance, electronic warfare and jamming operations. The Prowler is carried on all classes of the US Aircraft Carrier fleet: *Enterprise*, *Nimitz*, *Kitty Hawk*, *John F. Kennedy* and *Forrestal*. Its primary naval role is to protect US or allied carrier groups and aircraft by countering hostile radar and jamming enemy communications. It also carries out electronic surveillance tasks and provides defence against incoming anti-ship missiles. The aircraft is crewed by a pilot and three electronic counter-measures (ECM) officers. The forward section of the cockpit accommodates the pilot on the port side and one ECM officer station equipped with the communications and navigation systems, and the defensive ECM including the decoy dispensers. The rear cockpit accommodates two ECM officers and the ALQ-99 control and display stations. The Prowler carries five ALQ-99 tactical jamming pods, two under each wing and one under the fuselage. Each pod houses two powerful continuous wave (CW) transmitters which use beam steering to direct the jamming signal at the threat.

SPECIFICATIONS

Primary Role:	*electronic warfare*
Crew:	*4*
Contractor:	*Grumman*
Length:	*17.98m (59ft)*
Wingspan:	*16.15m (53ft)*
Height:	*4.57m (15ft)*
Maximum Take-off Weight:	*27,954kg (61,500lb)*
Powerplant:	*2 x Pratt & Whitney J52-P408 turbofans*
Thrust:	*5090kg (11,200lb) each*
Maximum Speed:	*976km/h (610mph)*
Ceiling:	*12,192m (40,000ft)*
Range:	*1563km (977 miles)*
Armament:	*four hardpoints for HARM (High Speed Anti-Radiation Missile)*
Systems:	*ALQ-99F tactical jammer*
Date Deployed:	*1977*

EC-130H COMPASS CALL/RIVET FIRE

Compass Call is the designation for a modified version of Lockheed's C-130 Hercules aircraft configured to perform tactical command, control and communications countermeasures (C3CM). Targeting command and control systems provides commanders with an immense advantage both before and during air operations. Compass Call provides a non-lethal means of denying and disrupting enemy command and control, degrading his combat capability and reducing losses to friendly forces. Modifications to the aircraft include an electronic countermeasures system (Rivet Fire), an air refuelling capability and associated navigation and communications systems. Compass Call is subject to worldwide deployment in support of tactical air/ground forces on very short notice. The Compass Call EC-130H is flown by the 355th Wing's 41st and 43rd Electronic Combat Squadrons. Aided by the automated system, the crew analyze the signal environment, designate targets and ensure the system is operating effectively. In a war situation, a signal may be received and linguists on board the aircraft analyze it to determine if it is an enemy signal. If there is a threat, enemy communications would be jammed. On the back of the aircraft is microwave-powered equipment which sends out high-energy radio frequency or interference.

SPECIFICATIONS

Primary Role:	*control and communications countermeasures*
Crew:	*13*
Contractor:	*Lockheed Martin*
Length:	*29.7m (97.75ft)*
Wingspan:	*40.41m (132.6ft)*
Height:	*11.6m (38.25ft)*
Maximum Take-off Weight:	*79,545 kg (175,000lb)*
Powerplant:	*4 x Allison T56-A-15 turboprops*
Thrust:	*6724kg (14,793lb) each*
Maximum Speed:	*602km/h (376mph)*
Ceiling:	*10,060m (33,005ft)*
Range:	*8793km (5496 miles)*
Armament:	*none*
Systems:	*electronic countermeasures system*
Date Deployed:	*1986*

ES-3A SHADOW

The ES-3A is a high-winged, twin-engine, carrier-based electronic reconnaissance mission aircraft equipped with folding wings, a launch bar and tailhook. The heart of the Shadow is an avionics suite based on the Aries II system of the land-based EP-3E Orion. The Shadow's fuselage is packed with sensor stations and processing equipment, and the exterior sports over 60 antennae. The ES-3A Shadow crew is comprised of two pilots and two systems operators. Advanced sensor, navigation and communications systems allow the Shadow's crew to collect extensive data and distribute high-quality information through a variety of channels to the carrier battle group. This gives the battle group commander a clear picture of potential airborne, surface and sub-surface threats. Missions flown by the detachment include over-the-horizon targeting, strike support and reconnaissance. All 16 ES-3 aircraft are essentially modified S-3 Viking airframes, whose submarine detection and other maritime surveillance equipment was removed and the weapons bay fitted with avionics racks to accommodate the ES-3's sensors. The first ES-3A was delivered in 1991. In 1998, the navy made the decision to retire the Shadow early, due to cost implications. All Shadows are now in storage, but may return to service in the future.

SPECIFICATIONS

Primary Role:	*electronic warfare*
Crew:	*4*
Contractor:	*Lockheed Martin*
Length:	*16.26m (53.3ft)*
Wingspan:	*20.93m (68.6ft)*
Height:	*6.93m (22.75ft)*
Maximum Take-off Weight:	*23,882kg (52,540lb)*
Powerplant:	*2 x General Electric TF34-GE-2 turbofans*
Thrust:	*4516kg (9935lb) each*
Maximum Speed:	*814km/h (508mph)*
Ceiling:	*10,363m (34,000ft)*
Range:	*5560km (3475 miles)*
Armament:	*none*
Systems:	*full-spectrum RF receivers, DF equipment, inverse synthetic aperture radar, FLIR, ESM*
Date Deployed:	*1991*

F-14 TOMCAT

The F-14 Tomcat is the US Navy's carrier-based two-seat air defence, intercept, strike and reconnaissance aircraft. The variable-sweep wings and twin upright tail fins of the F-14 Tomcat give the aircraft its distinctive appearance. The variable-sweep wings are set at 20 degrees for take-off, loitering and landing, and automatically change to a maximum sweep of 68 degrees, which reduces drag for high subsonic to supersonic speeds. The wings are swept at 75 degrees for aircraft carrier stowage. The F-14 is armed with a General Electric Vulcan M61A-1 20mm gun with 675 rounds of ammunition, which is mounted internally in the forward section of the fuselage on the port side. The aircraft has eight hardpoints for carrying ordnance, four on the fuselage and two each side under the fixed section of the wings. The aircraft was developed by Northrop Grumman to replace the F-4 Phantom fighter and entered service with the US Navy in 1972. In 1987 the F-14B with an upgraded engine went into production. Further upgrades to the aircraft's radar, avionics and missile capability resulted in the F-14D Super Tomcat which first flew in 1988. The US Navy currently operates 338 F-14 aircraft of all three variants. The aircraft continues to receive phased improvements and is due to remain in service until 2007.

SPECIFICATIONS

Primary Role:	carrier-based multirole fighter
Crew:	2
Contractor:	Grumman Aerospace
Length:	18.6m (61.75ft)
Wingspan:	19m (64ft) to 11.4m (38ft)
Height:	4.8m (16ft)
Maximum Take-off Weight:	32,805kg (72,900lb)
Powerplant:	2 x F-110-GE-400 turbofans
Thrust:	12,150kg (27,000lb) each
Maximum Speed:	2470km/h (1544mph)
Ceiling:	16,154m (53,000ft)
Range:	2965km (1853 miles)
Armament:	1 x 20mm cannon; 4 x AIM-7 or 4 x AIM-54; 4 x AIM-9 or 2 x AIM-9 and 2 x AIM-7
Systems:	AN/APG-71, TARPS, AN/ALE-39 & 29
Date Deployed:	1972

F-15C EAGLE

The F-15 Eagle is an all-weather, highly manoeuvrable tactical fighter designed to gain and maintain air superiority in air combat. The Eagle's air superiority is achieved through a mixture of manoeuvrability, acceleration, range, weapons and avionics. It has electronic systems and weaponry to detect, acquire, track and attack enemy aircraft while operating in friendly or enemy controlled airspace. Its weapons and flight control systems are designed so one person can safely and effectively perform air-to-air combat. It can penetrate enemy defences, outperform and outfight current or projected enemy aircraft. The F-15's superior manoeuvrability and acceleration are achieved through high engine thrust-to-weight ratio and low-wing loading. Low wing-loading (the ratio of aircraft weight to its wing area) is a vital factor in manoeuvrability and, combined with the high thrust-to-weight ratio, enables the F-15 to turn tightly without losing speed. The F-15C is an improved version of the original F-15A single-seat air superiority fighter. Additions incorporated into the F-15C include upgrades to the avionics as well as increased internal fuel capacity and a higher allowable gross take-off weight. The F-15C has an air combat victory ratio of 95:0, making it one of the most effective air superiority aircraft ever developed.

SPECIFICATIONS

Primary Role:	*tactical fighter*
Crew:	*1*
Contractor:	*McDonnell Douglas*
Length:	*19.43m (63.75ft)*
Wingspan:	*13.05m (42.75ft)*
Height:	*5.63m (18.47ft)*
Maximum Take-off Weight:	*36,741kg (81,000lb)*
Powerplant:	*2 x F100-P-220 turbofans*
Thrust:	*10,659kg (23,450lb) each*
Maximum Speed:	*2655km/h (1659mph)*
Ceiling:	*18,290m (60,000ft)*
Range:	*5745km (3590 miles)*
Armament:	*1 x M-61A1 20mm gun, 4 x AIM-9L/M and 4 x AIM-7F/M*
Systems:	*AN/APG-70 radar, IFF, AN/ALQ-135(V), AN/ALQ-128, RWR, AN/AVQ-26, LANTIRN*
Date Deployed:	*1972*

F-15D EAGLE

The F-15D is a two-seat variant of the F-15C. The primary purpose of the F-15D is aircrew training, with an instructor occupying the rear seat while an upgrading pilot mans the front seat. A multi-mission avionics system sets the F-15 apart from other fighter aircraft. It includes a Head-Up Display (HUD), advanced radar, inertial navigation system, flight instruments, UHF communications, tactical navigation system and instrument landing system. It also has an internally mounted tactical electronic-warfare system, identification friend or foe (IFF) system, electronic countermeasures (ECM) set and a central digital computer. The HUD projects on the windscreen all essential flight information gathered by the integrated avionics system. This display, visible in any light conditions, provides the pilot with information necessary to track and destroy an enemy aircraft without having to look down at cockpit instruments. The F-15's radar can look up at high-flying targets and down at low-flying targets without being confused by ground clutter. It can also detect and track aircraft and small, high-speed targets at distances beyond visual range down to close range, and at altitudes down to tree-top level. For close-in dog fights, the radar automatically acquires enemy aircraft, and this information is projected on the HUD.

SPECIFICATIONS

Primary Role:	*tactical fighter*
Crew:	*2*
Contractor:	*McDonnell Douglas*
Length:	*19.43m (63.75ft)*
Wingspan:	*13.05m (42.75ft)*
Height:	*5.63m (18.47ft)*
Maximum Take-off Weight:	*36,741kg (81,000lb)*
Powerplant:	*2 x F100-P-220 turbofans*
Thrust:	*10,659kg (23,450lb) each*
Maximum Speed:	*2655km/h (1659mph)*
Ceiling:	*18,290m (60,000ft)*
Range:	*5745km (3590 miles)*
Armament:	*1 x M-61A1 20mm gun, 4 x AIM-9 and 4 x AIM-7*
Systems:	*AN/APG-70 radar, IFF, AN/ALQ-135(V), AN/ALQ-128, RWR, AN/AVQ-26, LANTIRN*
Date Deployed:	*1972*

F-15E STRIKE EAGLE

The F-15E is especially configured for the deep strike mission. The Strike Eagle accomplishes this mission by expanding on the capabilities of the air superiority F-15, adding a rear-seat weapon systems operator (WSO) crew member, and incorporating new avionics. The F-15E performs day and night all-weather air-to-air and air-to-ground missions including strategic strike and interdiction. Although primarily a deep interdiction platform, the F-15E can also perform close air support and escort missions. Strike Eagles are equipped with LANTIRN, enhancing night precision guided munitions (PGM) delivery capability. The F-15E inboard wing stations and the centerline can be loaded with various armaments. The outboard wing hardpoints are unable to carry heavy loads and are assigned for electronic countermeasures (ECM) pods. The other hardpoints can be employed for various loads with the use of multiple ejection racks (MERs). Each MER can hold six Mk 82 bombs or "Snakeye" retarded bombs, or six Mk 20 "Rockeye" dispensers, four CBU-52B, CBU-58B, or CBU-71B dispensers, or a single Mk 84 bomb. The F- 15E can also carry "smart" weapons: the CBU-10 laser-guided bomb based on the Mk 84 bomb, CBU-12, CBU-15 and AGM-65 Maverick air-to-ground missiles.

SPECIFICATIONS

Primary Role:	*long-range interdiction*
Crew:	*2*
Contractor:	*McDonnell Douglas*
Length:	*19.45m (63.8ft)*
Wingspan:	*13.05m (42.8ft)*
Height:	*5.64m (18.5ft)*
Maximum Take-off Weight:	*36,818kg (81,000lb)*
Powerplant:	*2 x F100-PW-229 turbofans*
Thrust:	*13,227kg (29,100lb) each*
Maximum Speed:	*2655km/h (1650mph)*
Ceiling:	*20,000m (65,000ft)*
Range:	*5600km (3500 miles)*
Armament:	*4 x AIM-9, 4 x AIM-7, AMRAAM); CBU-10, -12, -15 and -24, AGM-65, 1 x 20mm*
Systems:	*Raytheon AN/APG-70 synthetic aperture radar, HUD, LANTIRN*
Date Deployed:	*1987*

F-16C FIGHTING FALCON

The F-16 Fighting Falcon is a multirole fighter. It is highly manoeuvrable and has proven itself in air-to-air combat and air-to-surface attack. In an air combat role, the F-16's manoeuvrability and combat radius exceed that of all potential enemy fighter aircraft. It can locate targets in all-weather conditions and detect low-flying aircraft in radar ground clutter. The F-16 can fly more than 860km (500 miles), deliver its weapons with superior accuracy, defend itself against enemy aircraft, and return to its starting point. In designing the F-16, advanced aerospace science and proven reliable systems from other aircraft such as the F-15 and F-111 were selected. These were combined to simplify the aircraft and reduce its size, maintenance costs and weight. With a full load of internal fuel, the F-16 can withstand up to nine Gs – nine times the force of gravity – which exceeds the capability of other fighter aircraft. The cockpit and its bubble canopy give the pilot unobstructed forward and upward vision, and the seat-back angle was expanded from the usual 13 degrees to 30 degrees, increasing pilot comfort and gravity force tolerance. The pilot has excellent flight control of his F-16 through its "fly-by-wire" system. The F-16C is the current single-seat version of this excellent aircraft.

SPECIFICATIONS

Primary Role:	*multirole fighter*
Crew:	*1*
Contractor:	*Lockheed Martin*
Length:	*14.8m (48.55ft)*
Wingspan:	*9.8m (32.15ft)*
Height:	*4.8m (15.74ft)*
Maximum Take-off Weight:	*16,875kg (37,500lb)*
Powerplant:	*1 x F100-PW-229 turbofan*
Thrust:	*12,150kg (27,000lb)*
Maximum Speed:	*2400km/h (1500mph)*
Ceiling:	*15,000m (50,000ft)*
Range:	*3900km (2437 miles)*
Armament:	*1 x 20mm cannon, AMRAAM, AIM-7, AIM-9, AGM-88 HARM, Harpoon, Penguin*
Systems:	*RWR, Raytheon AN/ALQ-184, TACAN, IFF, FOTD*
Date Deployed:	*1979*

F-16D FIGHTING FALCON

The F-16D is the two-seat trainer version of the air-craft. Avionics systems include a highly accurate inertial navigation system in which a computer provides steering information to the pilot. The aircraft has UHF and VHF radios plus an instrument landing system. It also has a warning system and modular countermeasure pods to be used against airborne or surface electronic threats; the fuselage also has space for additional avionics systems. The Fibre Optic Towed Decoy (FOTD) provides aircraft protection against radar-guided missiles to supplement traditional radar-jamming equipment. The device is towed at varying distances behind the aircraft while transmitting a signal like that of a hostile radar. The missile will detect and lock onto the decoy rather than the aircraft. This is achieved by making the decoy's radiated signal stronger than that of the aircraft. The F-16C and F-16D aircraft, which are the single- and two-seat counterparts to the earlier F-16A and B, incorporate the latest cockpit control and display technology. All F-16s delivered since November 1981 have built-in structural and wiring provisions and systems architecture that permit expansion of the aircraft's multirole flexibility to perform precision strike, night attack and beyond-visual-range interception missions.

SPECIFICATIONS

Primary Role:	*multirole fighter*
Crew:	*2*
Contractor:	*Lockheed Martin*
Length:	*14.8m (48.56ft)*
Wingspan:	*9.8m (32.15ft)*
Height:	*4.8m (16ft)*
Maximum Take-off Weight:	*17,045kg (37,500lb)*
Powerplant:	*1 x F100-PW-229 turbofan*
Thrust:	*12,150kg (27,000lb)*
Maximum Speed:	*2400km/h (1500mph)*
Ceiling:	*15,000m (50,000ft)*
Range:	*3900km (2437 miles)*
Armament:	*1 x 20mm cannon, AMRAAM, AIM-7, AIM-9 AAMs, HARM; Harpoon, Penguin*
Systems:	*AN/ALR-56M, Elta EL/L-8240 ECM, TACAN, FOTD*
Date Deployed:	*1979*

F/A-18 HORNET

The F/A-18 Hornet is a single- and two-seat, twin engine, multi-mission fighter/attack aircraft that can operate from either aircraft carriers or land bases. The F/A-18 fills a variety of roles: air superiority, fighter escort, suppression of enemy air defences, reconnaissance, forward air control, close and deep air support, and day and night strike missions. The F/A-18 has a digital control-by-wire flight control system which provides excellent handling qualities, and allows pilots to learn to fly the aircraft with relative ease. At the same time, this system provides exceptional manoeuvrability and allows the pilot to concentrate on operating the weapons system. Following a successful run of more than 400 A and B models, the US Navy began taking fleet deliveries of improved F/A-18C (single seat) and F/A-18D (dual seat) models in September 1987. These Hornets carry the Advanced Medium Range Air-to-Air Missile (AMRAAM) and the infrared imaging Maverick air-to-ground (AGM) missile. The multi-mission F/A-18E/F "Super Hornet" strike fighter is an upgrade of the combat-proven F/A-18C/D variant. Roll-out of the first Super Hornet occurred in September 1995, and it flew for the first time in November 1995. The specifications at right are for the C/D model.

SPECIFICATIONS

Primary Role:	*multirole attack aircraft*
Crew:	*1*
Contractor:	*McDonnell Douglas*
Length:	*17.07m (56ft)*
Wingspan:	*11.43m (37.5ft)*
Height:	*4.66m (15.28ft)*
Maximum Take-off Weight:	*25,401kg (56,000lb)*
Powerplant:	*2 x F404-GE-400 turbofans*
Thrust:	*14,545kg (32,000lb) each*
Maximum Speed:	*2082km/h (1301mph)*
Ceiling:	*15,240m (50,000ft)*
Range:	*3336km (2085 miles)*
Armament:	*1 x 20mm cannon; AMRAAM, SLAM, Harpoon, AGM-65; AGM-88 HARM*
Systems:	*IDECM, ALE-50 Towed Decoy, ALR-67(V)3 RWR, APG-73 radar*
Date Deployed:	*1983*

F-22 RAPTOR

The F-22 Raptor advanced tactical fighter aircraft is being developed for service with the US Air Force from the year 2005. During flight tests, the F-22 has demonstrated the ability to "supercruise": flying at sustained speeds of over Mach 1.5 without the use of afterburner. The F-22 construction is 39 percent titanium, 24 percent composite, 16 percent aluminum and 1 percent thermoplastic. Titanium is used for its high strength-to-weight ratio in critical stress areas, including some of the bulkheads, and also for its heat-resistant qualities in the hot sections of the aircraft. Carbon-fibre composites have been used for the fuselage frame, doors, intermediate spars on the wings, and for the honeycomb sandwich construction skin panels. The F119-100 low-bypass afterburning turbofan engine is the first fighter aircraft engine equipped with hollow, wide-chord fan blades. The total requirement is estimated to be 339 aircraft. The cockpit is fitted with hands-on throttle and stick (HOTAS) controls. The primary multifunction display provides a view of the air and ground tactical situation, including threat identity, threat priority and tracking information. Two other displays provide communication, navigation, identification and flight information. Three secondary displays show air and ground threat information.

SPECIFICATIONS

Primary Role:	*air superiority fighter*
Crew:	*1*
Contractor:	*Boeing/Lockheed Martin/ General Dynamics*
Length:	*18.90m (62.08ft)*
Wingspan:	*13.56m (44.5ft)*
Height:	*5.08m (16.67ft)*
Maximum Take-off Weight:	*27,216kg (60,000lb)*
Powerplant:	*2 x F119-PW-100 engines*
Thrust:	*15,909kg (35,000lb) each*
Maximum Speed:	*1600km/h (1000mph)*
Ceiling:	*unknown*
Range:	*unknown*
Armament:	*AIM-9 Sidewinders; AMRAAM, 1 x 20mm gun, JDAM*
Systems:	*AN/APG-77, RWR, JTIDS, identification friend or foe (IFF)*
Date Deployed:	*2005 (estimate)*

F-117A NIGHTHAWK

The F-117A Nighthawk is the world's first operational aircraft designed to exploit low-observable stealth technology. The size of an F-15 Eagle, it is powered by two General Electric F404 turbofan engines and has quadruple-redundant fly-by-wire flight controls. Air refuelable, it supports worldwide commitments and adds to the deterrent strength of US military forces. The F-117A can employ a variety of weapons, and is equipped with sophisticated navigation and attack systems integrated into an advanced digital avionics suite that increases mission effectiveness and reduces pilot workload. Detailed planning for missions into highly defended target areas is accomplished by an automated mission planning system developed to take advantage of the unique capabilities of the F-117A. The 49th Fighter Wing serves as the only F-117 Home Station, and provides full flightline maintenance capabilities as well as back-shop support, and the 49th Operations Group operates and maintains the F-117A aircraft. The 8th and 9th Fighter Squadrons are designated to employ the F-117A Nighthawk in combat. The F-117 usually deploys in support of contingency operations, as directed by National Command Authorities. Depending on the deployment duration, varying levels of extra maintenance support may also be deployed.

SPECIFICATIONS

Primary Role:	fighter/attack
Crew:	1
Contractor:	Lockheed Martin
Length:	20.3m (66.6ft)
Wingspan:	13.3m (43.63ft)
Height:	3.8m (12.46ft)
Maximum Take-off Weight:	23,814kg (52,500lb)
Powerplant:	2 x F404-GE turbofans
Thrust:	9818kg (21,600lb) each
Maximum Speed:	1040km/h (646mph)
Ceiling:	unknown
Range:	unlimited with refuelling
Armament:	Paveway II, Paveway III, BLU 109, WCMD, B61
Systems:	FLIR, DLIR, AP-102 mission control, IRADS
Date Deployed:	1982

JOINT STRIKE FIGHTER

The F-35 is the result of the US Defense Department's Joint Strike Fighter (JSF) programme, which sought to build a multirole fighter optimized for the air-to-ground role, designed to meet the needs of the air force, navy, Marine Corps and allies within cost affordability, with improved survivability, precision engagement capability, the mobility necessary for future joint operations, and the reduced life-cycle costs associated with future defence budgets. By using many of the same technologies developed for the F-22, the F-35 will be able to capitalize on commonality and modularity to maximize affordability. Lockheed Martin, the eventual winner of the JSF competition, developed four versions of the Joint Strike Fighter to fulfil the needs of the US armed forces and Great Britain's Royal Air Force and Royal Navy. All versions have the same fuselage and internal weapons bay, plus common outer mold lines with similar structural geometries, identical wing sweeps, and comparable tail shapes. The weapons are stored in two parallel bays located aft or rear of the main landing gear. The canopy, radar, ejection system, subsystems and avionics are all common among the different versions. The same core engine, based on the F119 built by Pratt & Whitney, powers the different versions of the F-35.

SPECIFICATIONS

Primary Role:	*strike fighter*
Crew:	*1*
Contractor:	*Lockheed Martin*
Length:	*13.71m (45ft)*
Wingspan:	*10.97m (36ft)*
Height:	*unknown*
Maximum Take-off Weight:	*22,727kg (50,000lb)*
Powerplant:	*1 x JSF119-611 turbofan*
Thrust:	*15,909kg (35,000lb)*
Maximum Speed:	*unknown*
Ceiling:	*unknown*
Range:	*1120km (700 miles)*
Armament:	*unknown*
Systems:	*AESA radar, ECM, electro-optical targeting system, DAIRS, HUD*
Date Deployed:	*2008*

KC-10A EXTENDER

The KC-10A tanker/cargo aircraft carries out its missions without dependence on overseas bases and without depleting critical fuel supplies in the theatre of operations. Equipped with its own refuelling receptacle, it can support the deployment of fighters, fighter support aircraft and airlifters from US bases to anywhere in the world. The aerial refuelling capability of the KC-10A nearly doubles the non-stop range of a fully loaded C-5 strategic transport. In addition, its cargo capability enables the United States to deploy fighter squadrons and their unit support personnel and equipment with a single aircraft type, instead of requiring both tanker and cargo variants. The US Air Force calls the KC-10A the "Extender" because of its ability to carry out aerial refuelling and cargo mission without forward basing, thus extending the mobility of US forces. To facilitate the handling of cargo, the KC-10A is equipped with a versatile system to accommodate a broad spectrum of loads. The system, adapted in part from the commercial DC-10, has been enhanced with the addition of powered rollers, powered winch provisions for assistance in the fore and aft movement of cargo, an extended ball mat area to permit loading of larger items, and cargo pallet couplers that allow palletizing of cargo items too large for a single pallet.

SPECIFICATIONS

Primary Role:	aerial refuelling/transport
Crew:	4
Contractor:	Douglas Aircraft
Length:	54.4m (178.47)
Wingspan:	50m (164ft)
Height:	17.4m (57ft)
Maximum Take-off Weight:	265,500kg (590,000lb)
Powerplant:	3 x General Electric CF-6-50C2 turbofans
Thrust:	23,625kg (52,500lb) each
Maximum Speed:	990km/h (619mph)
Ceiling:	12,727m (42,000ft)
Range:	7040km (4400 miles)
Armament:	none
Systems:	advanced aerial refuelling boom
Date Deployed:	1981

KC-130

The KC-130 is a multirole tactical tanker/transport which provides the support to US Marine Air Ground Task Forces. It provides inflight refuelling to both tactical aircraft and helicopters as well as rapid ground refuelling when required. Additional tasks performed are aerial delivery of troops and cargo, emergency re-supply into unimproved landing zones within the objective or battle area, airborne Direct Air Support Centre, emergency medevac, tactical insertion of combat troops and equipment, evacuation missions, and support of special operations. The KC-130 is equipped with a removeable 136.26-litre (3600-gallon) steel fuel tank that is carried inside the cargo compartment. The two wing-mounted hose and drogue refuelling pods each transfer up to 1135.5 litres (300 gallons) per minute to two aircraft simultaneously, allowing for rapid cycle times of multiple-receiver aircraft formations (typically four aircraft in less than 30 minutes). Some KC-130s are also equipped with defensive electronic and infrared countermeasures systems. Development is currently under way for the incorporation of night vision lighting, night vision goggle, head-up displays, global positioning system, and jam-resistant radios. The new KC-130J is capable of inflight refuelling of both fixed- and rotary wing aircraft.

SPECIFICATIONS

Primary Role:	*inflight refuelling; tactical transport*
Crew:	*6*
Contractor:	*Lockheed Martin*
Length:	*29.79m (97.75ft)*
Wingspan:	*40.39m (132.6ft)*
Height:	*11.68m (38.3ft)*
Maximum Take-off Weight:	*79,450kg (175,000lb)*
Powerplant:	*4 x T56-A-16 turboprops*
Thrust:	*6724kg (14,793lb) each*
Maximum Speed:	*580km/h (362.25mph)*
Ceiling:	*9140m (30,000ft)*
Range:	*1840km (1150 miles)*
Armament:	*none*
Systems:	*defensive electronic and infrared countermeasures systems*
Date Deployed:	*1962*

KC-135R STRATOTANKER

The KC-135 Stratotanker's primary mission is to refuel long-range bombers. The primary air fuel transfer method is through the tanker's flying boom, controlled by an operator stationed at the rear of the fuselage. A shuttlecock drogue can be trailed behind the boom and used to refuel aircraft equipped with refuelling probes. About 45 US Air Force KC-135R Stratotankers are fitted with Mark 32B wingtip hose and drogue air refuelling pods, which are capable of refuelling US Navy and NATO aircraft which use a probe and drogue system instead of a boom and receptacle. The receiving aircraft approaches the tanker and its probe makes contact with a hose reeled out and trailing from the tanker. The installation of wingtip refuelling pods involves a major modification and refit to the entire aircraft, including modifications to the wing and fuselage fuel tanks, additional fuel-control systems and the installation of indicators and circuit breakers on the flight deck. Inside the refuelling pods, a collapsible funnel-shaped drogue is attached to a hose which is reeled out to trail behind the wing of the aircraft. The hose is fitted with a constant tension spring to give stability to it while it is extended. The F108 turbofans are very fuel efficient, which allows the aircraft to transport more fuel for other aircraft over farther distances.

SPECIFICATIONS

Primary Role:	*aerial refuelling*
Crew:	*4*
Contractor:	*Boeing*
Length:	*40.8m (136.25ft)*
Wingspan:	*39.2m (130.8ft)*
Height:	*11.5m (38.3ft)*
Maximum Take-off Weight:	*146,590kg (322,500lb)*
Powerplant:	*4 x F108-CF-100 turbofans*
Thrust:	*10,000kg (22,224lb) each*
Maximum Speed:	*976km (610mph)*
Ceiling:	*15,152m (50,000ft)*
Range:	*17,907km (11,192 miles)*
Armament:	*none*
Systems:	*FMS-800 integrated flight management system, TCAS, EGPWS, Integrated Processing Centres*
Date Deployed:	*1965*

MC-130E/H COMBAT TALON

The mission of the MC-130E Combat Talon I and MC-130H Combat Talon II is to provide global, day, night and adverse weather capability to airdrop and airland personnel and equipment in support of US Special Forces. The MC-130H conducts infiltrations into politically denied/sensitive defended areas to re-supply or exfiltrate special operations forces and equipment. These aircraft are equipped with inflight refuelling equipment, terrain-following, terrain-avoidance radar, an inertial and global positioning satellite navigation system, and a high-speed aerial delivery system. The special navigation and aerial delivery systems are used to locate small drop zones and deliver people or equipment with greater accuracy and at higher speeds than possible with a standard C-130. Nine of the MC-130Es are equipped with the surface-to-air Fulton air recovery system. It involves use of a large, helium-filled balloon used to raise a nylon lift line. The MC-130E flies towards the lift line at 240km/h (150mph), snags it with scissors-like arms located on the aircraft nose and the person or item of equipment is lifted off, experiencing less shock than that caused by a parachute opening. Aircrew members then use a hydraulic winch to pull the person or equipment aboard the aircraft through the open rear cargo door.

SPECIFICATIONS

Primary Role:	*support of special operations*
Crew:	*4 or 5*
Contractor:	*Lockheed Martin*
Length:	*MC-130E, 30.7m (100.8ft); MC-130H, 30.4m (99.75ft)*
Wingspan:	*40.4m (132.6ft)*
Height:	*11.7m (38.5ft)*
Maximum Take-off Weight:	*70,454kg (155,000lb)*
Powerplant:	*4 x T56-A-15 turboprops*
Thrust:	*6724kg (14,793lb) each*
Maximum Speed:	*480km/h (300mph)*
Ceiling:	*10,000m (33,000ft)*
Range:	*4976km (3110 miles)*
Armament:	*none*
Systems:	*AN/APQ-170 radar, narrow band SATCOM (NBS), DAMA modems, SINCGARS, ACP*
Date Deployed:	*1966*

P-3C ORION

The P-3A was first operational in the United States Navy in 1962. The P-3C version entered service in 1969 and has been continuously upgraded and updated with new avionics systems and mission equipment. The aircraft is flown on missions up to 14 hours long. The flight deck accommodates the pilot, the co-pilot and the flight engineer. The main cabin is configured as a mission operations room for the tactical coordinator, the navigator and communications operator, two operators for the acoustic sensor suite, the electromagnetic sensors systems operator (responsible for the operation of the radar, electronic support measures, infrared detection system and magnetic anomaly detectors), the ordnance crew member and the flight technician. Circular protruding windows in the main cabin give the crew a 180-degree view. The aircraft can carry weapons in the bomb bay and on 10 underwing pylons. The bomb bay is in the underside of the fuselage forward of the wing. US Navy P-3C aircraft are equipped to carry the Harpoon AGM-84 anti-ship and stand-off land attack missile. More than 700 P-3 aircraft have been built by Lockheed Martin. It carries the United States Navy designation P-3, the Canadian Forces designations CP-140 Aurora and the CP-140A Arcturus, and the Spanish designation P-3.

SPECIFICATIONS

Primary Role:	*maritime patrol and anti-submarine warfare*
Crew:	*11*
Contractor:	*Lockheed Martin*
Length:	*35.61m (116.8ft)*
Wingspan:	*30.37m (99.6ft)*
Height:	*10.27m (33.7ft)*
Maximum Take-off Weight:	*61,235kg (134,717lb)*
Powerplant:	*4 x T56-A-14 turboprops*
Thrust:	*3661kg (8054lb) each*
Maximum Speed:	*760km/h (475mph)*
Ceiling:	*8500m (27,887ft)*
Range:	*3800km (2375 miles)*
Armament:	*Harpoon, SLAM, AGM 65, MK-46/50 torpedoes, mines*
Systems:	*AN/APS-137(V), AN/ARR-78(V), ASQ-81, ASA-65, ALQ-78(V)*
Date Deployed:	*1962*

RC-135 RIVET JOINT

The basic airframe of the RC-135 resembles that of the slightly larger Boeing 707 from which it is derived. The interior seats 32 people, including the cockpit crew, electronic warfare officers, intelligence operators and inflight maintenance technicians. The Rivet Joint's modifications are primarily related to its on-board sensor suite, which allows the mission crew to detect, identify and geolocate signals throughout the electromagnetic spectrum. The mission crew can then forward gathered information in a variety of formats to a wide range of consumers via Rivet Joint's extensive communications suite. Having a long service career, RC-135s originally flew from remote bases in Alaska and elsewhere to collect data on Soviet ballistic missile testing during the Cold War. With the use of passive sensors, the RC-135 gathers imagery intelligence (IMINT), telemetry intelligence (TELINT), and signals intelligence (SIGINT). The present RC-135 fleet of 21 aircraft currently consists of four varieties: two RC-135S Cobra Ball, one RC-135X Cobra Eye, two RC-135U Combat Sent, 14 RC-135V/W Rivet Joint, and two RC-135 trainers. The types are assigned to the USAF's 55th Wing, Nebraska. RC-135s saw action during the 1991 Gulf War, supplying intelligence through datalink to AWACS and navy command ships.

SPECIFICATIONS

Primary Role:	*signals intelligence collection*
Crew:	*32*
Contractor:	*Raytheon*
Length:	*41.1m (135ft)*
Wingspan:	*39.9m (131ft)*
Height:	*12.8m (42ft)*
Maximum Take-off Weight:	*133,633kg (297,000lb)*
Powerplant:	*4 x TF33-P-5 turbofans*
Thrust:	*7295kg (16,050lb) each*
Maximum Speed:	*800km/h (500mph)*
Ceiling:	*12,725m (41,750ft)*
Range:	*6500km (4063 miles)*
Armament:	*none*
Systems:	*UHF, VHF, HF, and SATCOM communications, Tactical Digital Information Link, TIBS*
Date Deployed:	*1964*

S-3B VIKING

S-3B aircraft are tasked by carrier battle group commanders to provide anti-submarine warfare and anti-surface warfare, surface surveillance and intelligence collection, electronic warfare, mine warfare, coordinated search and rescue, and fleet support missions, including air wing tanking. The S-3B is a modified S-3A anti-submarine warfare aircraft which has anti-surface warfare capabilities through improvements to various mission avionics and armament systems. It has increased capabilities through improvements to the general-purpose digital computer, acoustic data processor, radar, sonobuoy receiver, sonobuoy reference system, electronic support measures and includes the installation of an electronic countermeasures dispensing system. The S-3B's high-speed computer system processes information generated by the acoustic and non-acoustic target sensor systems. This includes a new inverse synthetic aperture radar. To destroy targets, the Viking employs an impressive array of airborne weaponry. This provides the fleet with a very effective airborne capability to combat the significant threat presented by modern combatants and submarines. Additionally, all S-3B aircraft are capable of carrying an inflight refuelling "buddy" store. This allows the transfer of fuel from the Viking aircraft to other naval aircraft.

SPECIFICATIONS

Primary Role:	*anti-submarine/surveillance*
Crew:	*4*
Contractor:	*Lockheed Martin*
Length:	*16.3m (53.3ft)*
Wingspan:	*20.9m (68.6ft)*
Height:	*6.9m (22.75ft)*
Maximum Take-off Weight:	*21,592kg (47,502lb)*
Powerplant:	*2 x TF-34-GE-400B turbofans*
Thrust:	*8432kg (18,550lb) each*
Maximum Speed:	*834km/h (521mph)*
Ceiling:	*12,192m (40,000ft)*
Range:	*6085km (3803 miles)*
Armament:	*AGM-84, AGM-65 , torpedoes, mines, rockets, bombs*
Systems:	*GPS, MR/RS, UHR/SAR, JTIDS, RTSDL, AN/AYK-23 Digital Computer, EO/IR sensor*
Date Deployed:	*1975*

T-38 TALON

The T-38 Talon is a twin-engine, high-altitude, supersonic jet trainer used in a variety of roles because of its design, economy of operations, ease of maintenance, high performance and exceptional safety record. It is used primarily by the Air Education and Training Command for undergraduate pilot and pilot instructor training. Air Combat Command, Air Mobility Command and the National Aeronautics and Space Administration also use the T-38 in various roles. The T-38 has swept-back wings, a streamlined fuselage and tricycle landing gear with a steerable nose wheel. Two independent hydraulic systems power the ailerons, flaps, rudder and other flight-control surfaces. The instructor and student sit in tandem on rocket-powered ejection seats in a pressurized, air-conditioned cockpit. Critical components are waist high and can thus be easily reached by maintenance crews. Student pilots fly the T-38A to learn supersonic techniques, formations, night and instrument flying and cross-country navigation. More than 60,000 pilots have earned their wings in the T-38A. Test pilots and flight test engineers are trained in the T-38A at the US Air Force Test Pilot School at Edwards Air Force Base. The Air Force Material Command uses T-38As to test experimental equipment such as electrical and weapon systems.

SPECIFICATIONS

Primary Role:	*advanced jet pilot trainer*
Crew:	*2*
Contractor:	*Northrop Corporation*
Length:	*14m (46.3ft)*
Wingspan:	*7.6m (25.25ft)*
Height:	*3.8m (12.46ft)*
Maximum Take-off Weight:	*5670kg (12,500lb)*
Powerplant:	*2 x J85-GE-5 turbojets*
Thrust:	*1315kg (2900lb) each*
Maximum Speed:	*1299km/h (812mph)*
Ceiling:	*16,667m (55,000ft)*
Range:	*1600km (1000 miles)*
Armament:	*none*
Systems:	*GPS, ring-laser gyro-inertial navigation system, collision avoidance system, instrument-flight certified HUD*
Date Deployed:	*1961*

T-45 GOSHAWK

The T-45A Goshawk is the US Navy's two-seat advanced jet trainer. To meet the needs of the US Navy training mission and to ensure aircraft carrier compatibility, several modifications to the basic Hawk airframe were incorporated into the T-45 Goshawk design: new twin nose-wheel with catapult launch T-bar; nosewheel steering for manoeuvring within the confines of the carrier deck; strengthened airframe and undercarriage for catapult launches; relocated speed brakes; provision of under-fuselage tailhook; revised avionics; and modified cockpit layout for compatibility with frontline navy combat aircraft. The cockpit is air-conditioned and pressurized by an engine air-bleed system. The Head-Up Display (HUD) is fitted with a video camera system for post-mission analysis, primary and secondary air data indicators, and weapon-aiming computer and display. The aircraft is not armed but has a single pylon installed under each wing for carrying bomb racks, rocket pods or auxiliary fuel tanks. A single baggage pod can also be carried on the single fuselage centreline pylon. A gunsight supplied by CAI Industries is fitted in the rear cockpit. The US Navy has more than 100 T-45 Goshawks and a total of 234 is planned. The T-45TS pilot training scheme includes advanced simulators and computer-assisted instruction as well as training flight programmes.

SPECIFICATIONS

Primary Role:	*trainer*
Crew:	*2*
Contractor:	*Boeing/BAe*
Length:	*11.97m (39.25ft)*
Wingspan:	*9.38m (30.9ft)*
Height:	*4.27m (14ft)*
Maximum Take-off Weight:	*5909kg (12,758lb)*
Powerplant:	*1 x Adour Mk871 turbofan*
Thrust:	*2604kg (5730lb)*
Maximum Speed:	*1006km/h (625mph)*
Ceiling:	*12,192m (40,000ft)*
Range:	*1532km (958 miles)*
Armament:	*five hardpoints for carriage of training bombs and rockets*
Systems:	*AN/USN-2 AHRS, AN/ARN-144 range and instrument landing system, IFF*
Date Deployed:	*1992*

U-2R

The U-2 is a single-seat, single-engine reconnaissance aircraft which provides continuous day or night, high-altitude, all-weather, stand-off surveillance of an area in direct support of US and allied ground and air forces. Long, wide, straight wings give the U-2 glider-like characteristics. It can carry a variety of sensors and cameras, is an extremely reliable reconnaissance aircraft, and enjoys a high mission completion rate. However, the U-2 can be a difficult aircraft to fly due to its unusual landing characteristics: because of its high-altitude mission, the pilot must wear a full pressure suit. The U-2R, first flown in 1967, is 40 per-cent larger than the original U-2 designed by Kelly Johnson in the mid-1950s. Current U-2R models are being re-engined and will be designated as a U-2S/ST. The US Air Force accepted the first U-2S in October 1994. A tactical reconnaissance version, the TR-1A, first flew in August 1981 and was delivered to the air force the next month. Designed for stand-off tactical reconnaissance in Europe, the TR-1 was structurally identical to the U-2R. Operational TR-1As were used by the RAF's 17th Reconnaissance Wing beginning in February 1983. The last U-2 and TR-1 aircraft were deliv-ered to the US Air Force in October 1989. In 1992 all TR-1s and U-2s were redesignated U-2R.

SPECIFICATIONS

Primary Role:	high-altitude reconnaissance
Crew:	1
Contractor:	Lockheed Martin
Length:	19.2m (63ft)
Wingspan:	31.39m (103ft)
Height:	4.8m (16ft)
Maximum Take-off Weight:	18,598kg (41,000lb)
Powerplant:	1 x J75-PW-13B turbojet
Thrust:	7727kg (17,000lb)
Maximum Speed:	800km/h (500mph)
Ceiling:	27,432m (90,000ft)
Range:	6400km (4000 miles)
Armament:	none
Systems:	HR-329 (H-cam) camera, IRIS-III, SENIOR YEAR Defensive System, Airborne Information Transmission System
Date Deployed:	1955

VC-25A – AIR FORCE ONE

The mission of the VC-25A aircraft – Air Force One – is to provide transport for the president of the United States. The presidential air transport fleet consists of two specially configured Boeing 747-200B's – tail numbers 28000 and 29000 – with the designation VC-25A. When the president is aboard either aircraft, or any air force aircraft, the radio call sign is "Air Force One". Principal differences between the VC-25A and the standard Boeing 747, other than the number of passengers carried, are the electronic and communications equipment aboard, its interior configuration and furnishings, self-contained baggage loader, front and aft air stairs, and the capability for inflight refuelling. Accommodation for the president includes an executive suite consisting of a state room (with dressing room, lavatory and shower) and the president's office. A conference/dining room is also available for the president, his family and staff. Other separate accommodations are provided for guests, senior staff, Secret Service and security personnel, and the news media. Two galleys provide up to 100 meals at one sitting. Six passenger lavatories, including disabled access facilities, are provided as well as a rest area and mini-galley for the crew. The VC-25A also has a compartment outfitted with medical equipment and supplies for minor medical emergencies.

SPECIFICATIONS

Primary Role:	*presidential air transport*
Crew:	*26*
Contractor:	*Boeing*
Length:	*70.7m (231.8ft)*
Wingspan:	*59.6m (195.5ft)*
Height:	*19.3m (63.3ft)*
Maximum Take-off Weight:	*378,636kg (833,000lb)*
Powerplant:	*4 x CF6-80C2B1 turbofans*
Thrust:	*25,772kg (56,700lb) each*
Maximum Speed:	*1008km/h (630mph)*
Ceiling:	*13,746m (45,100ft)*
Range:	*12,480km (7800 miles)*
Armament:	*none*
Systems:	*multi-frequency radios for air-to-air, air-to-ground and satellite communications*
Date Deployed:	*1990*

INDEX

AA-8 Aphid AAM 40, 42, 43
AA-9 Amos AAM 43
AA-10 Alamo AAM 40, 42, 43, 44, 47
AA-11 Archer AAM 40, 43, 44
AA-12 Adder AAM 44
AAMs see air-to-air missiles
advanced electronically scanned array 84
AEW see airborne early warning
AEW&C see airborne early warning
   & control
AESA see advanced electronically
   scanned array
AGM-45 Shrike air-to-ground missile
   53
AGM-62 Walleye glide bomb 53
AGM-65 Maverick air-to-surface missile
   15, 16, 17, 25, 54
AGM-84 Harpoon ASM 28, 59
AGM-88 HARM see High-speed
   Anti-Radiation Missile
AGM-119 Penguin anti-ship missile 79
AGM-129 Advanced Cruise Missile 58
AIM-7 Sparrow AAM 30, 75
AIM-9 Sidewinder AAM 15, 16, 17, 21,
   25, 26, 26, 27, 28, 30, 33, 50, 53,
   56, 75, 76, 77, 80, 82
AIM-54 Phoenix AAM 75
AIM-120 advanced medium-range
   air-to-air missile 30, 50
Air-Launched Anti-Radar Missile 15,
   16, 17, 30
air-to-air missiles 7, 10, 19, 28, 30, 49,
   52
air-to-surface missiles 41, 45
airborne early warning 51
airborne early warning & control 34
Airborne Warning and Control System
   67, 71, 90
AIRPASS III Blue Parrot radar 24
ALARM see Air-Launched Anti-Radar
   Missile
ALQ-167 jamming suite 24
AMRAAM see AIM-120 advanced
   medium-range air-to-air missile
AN/AAR-44 infrared warning receiver
   55
AN/AAR-47 missile warning system
   55, 62
AN/ALQ 161A defensive avionics 57
AN/ALQ-184 radar 79
AN/APQ-170 radar 88
AN/APA-171 antenna 66
AN/APY-1/2 radar 67, 71
AN/APG-65 radar system 56
AN/APG-70 radar 76, 77, 78
AN/APS-145 radar 66
AN/UYG-70 advanced display system 66
angle rate bombing system 25, 56
anti-ship missiles 7

Apache air-to-ground missile 15, 16, 17
ARBS see angle rate bombing system
AS-7 Kerry air-to-ground missile 41, 42
AS-10 Karen air-to-ground missile 41,
   42
AS-11 Kilter air-to-ground missile 41
AS-12 Kegler air-to-ground missile 41
AS-13 Kingbolt air-to-ground missile 41
AS-14 Kedge air-to-ground missile 41,
   42
AS-16 Kickback short-range attack
   missile 46
AS.30L ASM 21
ASM-1 ASM 33
ASM-2 ASM 33
ASMP stand-off missile 18, 20, 22
ASMs see anti-ship missiles
ASMs see air-to-surface missiles
AWACS see Airborne Warning and
   Control System

C-180 missile 7
CAINS see carrier airborne inertial
   navigation system
CBU-52 bomb 54
CBU-58 bomb 54
CBU-71 bomb 54
CBU-87 bomb 54
CBU-89 bomb 54
CBU-99/100 cluster bomb 56
COMINT see communications
   intelligence
communications intelligence 12, 48

DAIRS see distributed aperture infrared
   sensor
DAMA see Demand Assigned Access
Demand Assigned Access 88
DLIR see downward-looking infrared
downward-looking infrared 83
dual mode tracker 25

E3 look-down radar 67
ECCM see electronic counter-counter
   measures
ECM see electronic countermeasures
electronic counter-counter measures 49
electronic countermeasures 10, 12, 14,
   21, 45, 47, 48, 49, 72, 77, 78, 80,
   84
electronic intelligence 11, 12, 48
electronic support measures 12, 27, 29,
   48, 74
ELINT see electronic intelligence
ESM see electronic support measures
Exocet ASM 21, 22, 23

Fibre Optic Towed Decoy 79. 80
FLIR see Forward-Looking Infrared
FMS-800 integrated flight management
   system 87
FOTD see Fibre Optic Towed Decoy
Forward-Looking Infrared 17, 25, 27,
   74, 83

GBU-12 laser-guided bomb 56
GBU-16 laser-guided bomb 56
GBU-24 Paveway laser-guided bomb
   15, 16, 17
Global Positioning System 11, 20, 30,
   91, 92
GPS see Global Positioning System

HARM see High Speed Anti-Radiation
   Missile
High-speed Anti-Radiation Missile 15,
   16, 17, 72, 79, 80, 81
Hsiung Feng II ASM 52

Identification Friend or Foe 53, 67, 76,
   77, 79, 82, 93
IFF see Identification Friend or Foe
imagery intelligence 90
IMINT see imagery intelligence
infrared acquisition and designation
   system 83
Infrared Search and Track system 13, 40
IRADS see infrared acquisition and
   designation system

JDAM see Joint Direct Attack Munition
Joint Direct Attack Munition 57
Joint Tactical Information Distribution
   System 15, 70, 82
JP233 anti-airfield weapon 16, 17

Kh-23 ASM 41, 42
Kh-25 ASM 41, 42
Kh-29 ASM 41, 42
Kh-55 ASM 45, 46

LANTIRN see low-altitude navigation
   and targeting infrared for night
LASTE see low altitude safety and
   enhancement
low-altitude navigation and targeting
   infrared for night 76, 77, 78
low altitude safety and enhancement 54

Magic 2 AAM 19
Magic R550 AAM 14, 21, 23
magnetic anomaly detector 27
Marine Air Ground Task Forces 86
Marine Air Support Detachment 63
Martel ASM 18
Mica AAM 22

National Command Authority 69

Patriot Missile System 62
Python AAM 32

R-35 AAM 42
R-27 AAM 40
R-60 AAM 42
Radar Warning Receiver 9, 10, 18, 21,
   40, 45, 47, 76, 77, 79, 82
RB71 AAM 49
RB74 AAM 49
RBS 15F ASM 49, 50
Royal Air Force 84
Royal Navy 84
RWR see Radar Warning Receiver

Sea Eagle ASM 16, 17, 30, 56
Shafrir AAM 32
short take-off and landing 12, 36, 48
SINCGARS see single channel ground
   and airborne radio system
single channel ground and airborne
   radio system 70
Sky Sword-II AAM 52
Skyflash missile 15
Sparrow AAM 33
STOL see short take-off and landing
Super 530 D AAM 19, 21

tactical airborne reconnaissance pod
   system 75
TARPS see tactical airborne
   reconnaissance pod system
Tri-Service Standoff Attack Missile 58
TSSAM see Tri-Service Standoff Attack
   Missile

vertical/short take-off and landing
   47, 56
V/STOL see vertical/short take-off
   and landing